JOHN COATES:
THE MAN WHO BUILT
THE SNOWMAN

Dedicated to my father, Norman Arthur, who sadly died before this book was published.

JOHN COATES: THE MAN WHO BUILT THE SNOWMAN

A biography of the producer of *The Snowman*, *Yellow Submarine* and many other films …

Written by Marie Beardmore
with an Epilogue by John Coates
Foreword by Raymond Briggs

British Library Cataloguing in Publication Data

John Coates: The Man Who Built *The Snowman*

A catalogue entry for this book is available from the British Library

ISBN: 9780 86196 682 0 (Paperback)

Published by
John Libbey Publishing Ltd, 3 Leicester Road, New Barnet, Herts EN5 5EW, United Kingdom
e-mail: john.libbey@orange.fr; web site: www.johnlibbey.com
Direct orders (UK and Europe): direct.orders@marston.co.uk

Distributed in Asia and N. America by **Indiana University Press**, 601 North Morton St,
Bloomington, IN 47404, USA. www.iupress.indiana.edu

Printed and bound in China by 1010 Printing International Ltd..

Contents

Excerpts from films on the accompanying DVD:

The Flying Man; *The Apple*; *Granpa*; *When the Wind Blows*;
The Tale of Peter Rabbit & Benjamin Bunny; *Famous Fred*;
The Wind in the Willows; *The Tailor of Gloucester*;
The Bear; *The Snowman*

Acknowledgements

Thanks to John first and foremost for allowing me to write his life story and for wanting to tell it warts and all, and to Giulietta, Nicola and Chris for their valuable co-operation.

Thanks to everyone who helped and supported me through this biography, which has been many years in the making. Special appreciation to my mum, father and brother for all their love and support over the years, and to Norman, Alex and Bella who have helped tremendously throughout the gestation of this book. To Apple Corp for their kind permission for use of The Beatles and *Yellow Submarine* images, Loraine for the beautiful cover image, Catherine and Samuel for their help with scanning the many photographs and Linda for her Photoshop expertise, a big thank you! A huge thank you to all those individuals and companies that supplied the many images in this book. Same to all the people who contributed stories and anecdotes about John; too many to mention here but you know who you are, and a very special thanks to Raymond Briggs for his funny and pithy foreword! Last but definitely not least, thanks to John Libbey for publishing. We got there in the end!

Preface

John and I have been friends ever since we met on a flight to Berlin for an industry event called Cartoon Movie over ten years ago. There's an intimacy to this book because it has developed over many years and over many interviews. It is a lot to trust someone to write your biography, your life story, and I thank John for trusting me enough to write his. We are from very different backgrounds; John is the upper-class nephew of J Arthur Rank and I'm a butcher's daughter from the Midlands, and, for me, understanding each other's lives has been a valuable part of the odyssey of writing this book.

John is a rare breed amongst animation producers these days, indeed amongst business people these days, with values that in some respects belong to a bygone age. In a communication-crazy world, he has a mobile phone but never uses it, doesn't know how to use a computer and only really conducts business over lunch.

Yet he gets his films made and not just any old films, but quality productions that stand the test of time, has won a plethora of awards, and values traditional ways of working, honesty, decency, fairness, that can seem outmoded in contemporary corporate life. He is indeed a very special man; *The Man Who Built the Snowman*, no less!

Facing page:
John and Marie
working hard on the
book in sunny Provence.
[© 2010 John Coates.]

Foreword

John Coates – "The Grandfather of British Animation". Some grandfather. Father of Wine, Women and Song, more like ... and not so much of the song, either. Wine, Women and Films, perhaps.

His shelves groaning under the weight of international awards, feted at festivals all over the world, John is also held in affectionate admiration by directors, animators and everyone in the industry. He is fawned over by restaurateurs because they know he understands about food and wine, having made a life-long study of the subject by decades of dedicated lunching.

It is during these famous lunches that all the negotiation is done. NO BUSINESS IN THE OFFICE is the rule. How many studios would have the nerve to do that? But then, John Coates is a larger than life character, normal rules do not apply.

Reading this fascinating biography we realise that he has packed in enough living to fill half a dozen lives. The huge projects he has taken on, often involving millions of pounds and at the same time having to deal with some very dodgy characters; this kind of life, even for a few weeks, would give most of us nervous breakdowns.

Facing page: Family Coates. John and Chris with dog. [© 2010 John Coates.]

Yet John has done it for decade after decade and always sails through these storms of financial complications and desperate anxieties to emerge serene, victorious and ready for another celebratory lunch. He has got his own way yet again and the resulting award-winning film proves he was right all along.

Today, incredibly, he is still at it! Now nearly a hundred years old, he drives to London almost every day, getting yet another couple of films going, before nipping out to lunch.

Reading this book about this super-human person may make you feel tired and want to go upstairs and lie down. But do not despair, you're not a failure, you're just not John Coates. After all, there can only be one.

Thank heaven for that.

Raymond Briggs
25 June 2010

1

Early Years

John Piesse Coates was born in 1927, between the wars. A good year for champagne! It was also a seminal year for communication, and heralded some big changes in media and technology. It was the year of the first ever Oscar, the first transatlantic phone call – New York City to London – and the year of the Jazz Singer, widely regarded as the first talking picture, which opened to rave reviews. That movie effectively killed the silent movie era; ironic considering that the wordless 'Snowman' was to make John more famous than any of his other films. How he made the transition from schoolboy to eventual celebrated producer has been a fabulous odyssey and the subject of this book.

John was fortunate enough to be born into wealth. His mother was the money because she was a Rank, the family that made its initial fortune from flour milling and later, Rank Films. As a young boy, John admired his entrepreneurial Uncle Jimmy, by all accounts an illustrious character. He was a millionaire even back then and John remembers him fondly as a man who enjoyed racing, had plenty of girlfriends and liked a drink. The impassioned Uncle Jimmy was a fun influence on his young nephew, who has forever kept a love of horses, pretty women and the odd tipple, and not necessarily in that order. John's Uncle Arthur, on the other hand, was a strict Methodist and teetotal, a way of life that proved an anathema to John.

In contrast to his well-heeled mother, John's father, Major Coates, came from more humble stock. He was a chartered surveyor by profession but had been a flyer during WWI, which had a profound influence on the young John who developed a life-long love of all things military. The Major's

1

army career ended abruptly when he was shot down in France by one of the much-feared Richthofen Circus, perhaps even by the infamous Red Baron himself. His plane tumbled into a shell hole and the wings stuck, cushioning his fall and saving his life, though he had a nasty gun shot wound on his leg afterwards.

One of four siblings, John was closer in age to his sister Anne (the Oscar winning film editor Anne V. Coates) than his older brothers, Michael and David. John and Anne shared a love of horses with their mother who kept show ponies and encouraged them to take part in competitions, in which they excelled. There were two major events: The International was held indoor at Olympia and Richmond Royal horse show was in the open air. Anne won the title champion rider of England (1938) and John claimed the crown the following year, 1939, age 12.

Anne was a rebel; she ran away from school at a young age and was always in trouble, which John loved because it kept the parental heat off him. David joined the family flour milling business, where the tradition was to work your way up from the factory floor, grafting, humping sacks of flour around. John was having none of that, though it was to be

Hunter Trials – 1940, Winter. John and Anne compete on their own ponies at the annual Easter Monday horse show and hunter trials at Scamperdale Farm, Edenbridge. Anne rides Cigarette and John rides Bruno. The bomb that went off near the family home killed both ponies not long afterwards. Their mum had show ponies but these two belonged to John and Anne. "We'd always had a pony each as we grew up, to do all the fun things and not the namby pamby stuff". [© 2010 John Coates.]

John stands with Princess Margaret and Princess Elizabeth, our future Queen, in the 1939 horse show at Olympia. John's mount, Kismet, won Champion pony at the event.

[© 2010 John Coates.]

many years before he followed his sister and joined the other family firm, Rank Films.

As a youngster, John lived in a bubble. He had a privileged life and thought having a houseful of servants and private grounds to run around in was the norm. His mother, better known affectionately in the family as "Pussyfoot" based on a 'wireless' character at the time, had a no-nonsense Yorkshire upbringing and ran the household and an army of staff with military efficiency. They lacked a butler, but the family seemed to have everything else: cook, maids and nannies, even an under nanny, a groom, a stable boy, a gardener and an under gardener, a chauffer and a mechanic. Over the years, "Pussy" managed all the domestic problems of her eccentric children as well as those of her many staff.

John's nanny, Evelyn, played a big part in his life. He was fond of his mum and dad, but it was Eve, as she was known, who looked after him in the years up to boarding school and to whom he was very attached. She worked on for his mother for many years and finally married Harris, the Head

Groom. They had two daughters who went on to start up a very successful equestrian centre of their own.

While John was still in short trousers, the family moved to the country to Crutchfield Farm, a small Elizabethan manor house near Gatwick. Here, he acquired his love of rural life and grew from boy to young man. The Coates had two farms, both dairy and several hundred acres between them, and had moved into the country "to be seen to be" according to John. The family never farmed them, of course, tenant farmers did that, but they were a godsend during the war years, providing lots of milk, chickens' eggs and guinea fowl.

He had a few years of bucolic peace before Germany had the affront to invade Poland, provoking the Second World War on September 1st 1939. Soon afterwards, John was given a four ten shot gun, complete with very long barrel and known as a poachers' gun. He had to keep the larder full of game, rabbits, partridges, pheasants, and often went out hunting with his dogs, an ill assorted team of Springer spaniel, a Dalmatian, hopeless until he trained it, and a Lurcher that Anne bought from gypsies. In the end, they became three intrepid hunting dogs and John spent many happy days in the fields catching his quarry – even the wealthy had to cope with rationing …

His family had to get used to the inconvenience of war. Although wealth kept things ticking along more normally than for people of moderate means, reality hit home when, one inevitable day, the air raid siren went off. In true blitz spirit and showing her Yorkshire mettle, John recalls his mum protesting: "I am not building an air raid shelter. If they're going to bomb me, they'll bomb me in my bed!" And that's almost what happened; a couple of months later, towards the end of the Battle of Britain, a stick of eight bombs fell alongside the family pile. It was quite a small blast, but it killed John's favourite pony and was strong enough to lift the door off its hinges and almost on to him.

As hostilities intensified and his siblings reached the age of conscription, each wanted to do their bit for king and country. On the day war broke out, John's older brother Michael went under the knife to get his rugby-bent nose straightened so he could pass the medical to be a fighter pilot. He never became a flier, but did enlist as an officer in the infantry, while David joined the RAF. John's parents had separated by then, so he felt quite alone when his brothers enlisted, and even more so when, later, Anne also left home to become a nurse. Desperately lonely and abandoned, a young man now and much wrapped up in things military, he had no choice but to find ways to amuse himself at home.

John lost his virginity in the summer of 1944. "I had to exercise my horse, and in the course of doing so I met a lady who joined me on rides. Her name was Susan and she was fairly grown up to me, probably 25. On one occasion, on a warm June day she said, 'why don't we tie the horses up?' And to my astonishment, she held my hand, and one thing led to another … The physical contact with the opposite sex was something I'd never experienced before, and she took charge. We both felt guilty in a funny sort of way, but we did meet a few times after. The problem was she had a husband fighting away in Italy at the time, but at least I'd learnt what it was all about and felt experienced when I went back to school next term."

School days

John's schooling was largely during the war. Prep school didn't shape him particularly but public school did. He was a pupil at the impressively progressive Stowe, once the home of the former Dukes of Buckingham; an idyllic place with grounds designed by 'Capability' Brown and beautiful buildings graced by fantastic woods, lakes and amazing temples. Unfortunately, the last Duke of Buckingham had been a little barmy; he went bankrupt and blew himself up, ironically in the Temple of Friendship, still in ruins to this day. The Duke had a taste for questionable large-scale projects: the third artificial lake had a porous soil and would not hold water, so he decided to line the whole thing with copper, a bold endeavor resulting in his financial ruin. There were also plans for building a straight road to his namesake Buckingham Palace; it goes into Buckingham town and is accurately aimed at Buckingham Palace, but never got down that far.

Stowe proffered an educational revolution for the wealthy and was far removed from the stuffier Eton and Harrow. A hundred parents fed up with the rigmarole of the old public school system decided to create something modern and started Stowe, which gave John his love of shape and form.

"We were surrounded by beauty and I don't care what anyone says, unless you're a Philistine it brushes off. Neoclassic bridges across the lake and the Temples of Friendship and the main centerpiece and colonnades with marvelous scenes, all influenced me a lot and made me realise something about aesthetics." His comments would have pleased Stowe's founder J.F. Roxburgh, whom history regards as the greatest public school head of the twentieth century. His vision was: "every pupil who goes out from Stowe will know beauty when he sees it, all the rest of his life".

Stowe School: John sits outside Grenville House, Stowe's North Front, during his first term at the school: "My study when I became senior was in the little window to the left". [© 2010 John Coates.]

Stowe's curriculum reflected its liberal ways; the place was more involved in the arts, music and sports than other schools of its ilk. After passing their school certificate, pupils were allowed to choose the games they wanted to play. Being a strong swimmer, John was a natural for water polo, but hated tennis and cricket, both popular 'summer' sports. He also played 'rugger' and made a good scrum half, playing in the second team, and acting as a reserve for the first. John's favourite subject was geography, mostly because he had a great teacher full of interesting ideas. He had a plan to irrigate the Sahara Desert by bulldozing a canal, 20 miles wide, from the Gulf of Libya in the Mediterranean all the

6

way to West Africa; this would let the sea flow through and make it rain, transforming the barren desert to fertile ground in no time at all.

Towards the end of his school days, John got a sharp reminder of the war raging around him. He was studying for his higher certificate when the Germans came. "I was sitting in a little window as dawn came up. This black plane came circling down quite low and I was just looking at it. As it turned, you could see there was a German cross on it. It was a Dornier bomber. That second, the bomb doors opened and the bombs fell out, but didn't hit the school. They bombed the rugby fields and the next one fell on the south run. They were only tiny bombs in the end." John still wonders if they knew they were bombing a school.

Stowe was not as strict as the older public schools, but not as degenerate as William Golding's *Lord of the Flies* either. Pupils carried around a pocket-sized red book with the school rules inside. Showing how times have changed, smoking was explained as a danger fire-wise and nothing to do with health. John, never goody two shoes, was caught smoking and got whacked by the headmaster – six of the best! Although bright, he was not extremely academic. He liked fighting and organised the inter-dormitory battles. Somebody once asked him what he would have done if he had not been a film producer. "I think I'd make a pretty-good general", he answered.

2

Army Years

John left the hallowed walls of Stowe in 1945; the war with Germany was over, but England and Japan were locked into a bloody and protracted battle, predicted to last as long as the German War had, at least four or five years. Before war interrupted, he was all set for Cambridge, but faced with the option of getting his degree or joining-up, John decided on the latter and signed up for three years in the armed-forces.

He coveted a place in the 11th Hussars elite cavalry regiment, once part of the brave Charge of the Light Brigade, but its commissioned ranks were limited to career soldiers not 'part-timers' like him. Usually, he would have been refused entry into the squad, but 'Pussy' came to the rescue: she knew the colonel, who pulled some strings for her son. John joined the 11th Hussars.

The army proved a life-changing experience for the young Coates, used to mingling in affluent society rather than with 'ordinary' folk. Army life started with six weeks basic training at Winchester Barracks. Like other new recruits, John, with brand-new kitbag, was nervous that first day and night. Next morning, he was kitted-out with standard issue battle dress and a rifle, without ammunition – that was allocated on the rifle range.

The tremendous sense of duty and seriousness of war prevailed heavily on him, like it did all the young men. None knew who would die for king and country, and as he looked around the barracks, a world away from Stowe aesthetics, he must have wondered if he would die young. After succumbing to initial feelings of isolation and loneliness, he managed to push maudlin thoughts aside. Showing flashes of the people skills that would make him such an adept producer, he adapted well to his new life, taking up fags and beer in the pub, like a regular 'bloke', though he had sneaked the odd cigarette at Stowe.

Training was rigorous and standard: bayonets, march up and down, boot polishing, be disciplined and do whatever you were told. The independent spirited young men who went in came out homogenous, identical of purpose, sense of self squashed. After all, on the battlefield, maverick thinking got you killed. John remembers having a go on the rifle range, but only after switching the helmet and face of the target from German to Japanese. Many years later, after completing *When The Wind Blows*, the anti-nuclear war film directed by Jimmy Murakami, he told that story on Japanese television. "The Japanese news people understood what I was saying: all is well that ends well or something like that."

After the six weeks training, recruits went to their next section – tanks for John. He was sent to the 57th training regiment, Catterick, Yorkshire, where it was so cold the bedsteads had frost on them. He shared an up and down bunk with a Geordie; they became good friends and learnt to understand each other "down the pub". Nine months later, he was selected for officer cadet training. By now he had learnt just about everything there was to know about a tank and could operate one with some panache.

Officer cadet training

Office training was another six weeks again of spit and polish, this time at the barracks in Aldershot; the guy in charge of the young cadets, Sergeant Major Brittain, had a voice so fierce he could march men a mile away. "He would stand right behind you and would shout in a high-pitched voice: "Am I hurting you!" And you'd say, "No sir!" And he'd say: "Well I should be because I'm standing on your hair – get it cut!"

The Sergeant Major had to defer to the young cadets because they above him in rank and John "still recalls the cynicism in his sir". After this training period, it was off to Battle Camp in North Wales, where it rained, constantly. "It was August. The men were a little optimistic that the weather might not be that bad", says John.

Battle Camp was meant to prepare the cadets for war

John middle row, centre, as officer cadet at Bovington Camp – OCTU. Officer Cadet Training Unit. [© 2010 John Coates.]

(though hostilities with Japan had by now ceased, following the US nuclear attacks on Nagasaki and Hiroshima, August 1945) so it was an intense period to build strength, stamina and to bring out their fighting spirit. John and his fellow cadets arrived at Bangor station in the pouring rain, where they were split into two companies. Each company climbed into a truck, tied down at the back so the men couldn't see outside. Like that, they journeyed up into the mountains. "It rained all the way, and the space of ground where we could lay out tents was sodden. But the tent was totally pointless because we were soaking wet anyway."

That first evening, the cadets were sent out in two men patrols "to make contact with the other side because they were the enemy". If they hadn't made "contact" within two hours, they were supposed to return to base. John remembers: "Me and another bloke headed off in pitch darkness in the middle of the mountains of North Wales, not knowing what the hell we were doing. We hadn't made contact with the 'enemy' so set off to get back to base. On the return journey, the guy I was with said it was my turn to go up over the next wall to try and find their camp. I remember stopping at the top and throwing a big rock …

There was silence and silence, then way down a final muffled splash. If I had gone over the wall, I would have been killed or maimed for life."

In shock, John and his partner found a narrow track and made their way back to base, only to find many casualties from that exercise – some men had hurled rocks at each other (the enemy) and were suffering for it. John was at his peak of physical fitness then; all the soldiers had to be, just to make them aware of battle conditions. One day he had to carry the mortar bombs and the stresses were close to fighting a real enemy. "I asked someone to help me with them over a wall, and he just threw them at me in some kind of temper. The mortar bombs couldn't have gone off because they were not primed but that wasn't really the point ..."

For most of the camp, the men were divided into infantry sections of 7 or 8. Towards the end of the week, they were split into thirty men platoons. Each section had a Bren gun, a whole lot heavier than the standard rifle, so the men tossed coins to decide who got to carry it each day. John got lumbered with it during the final stages of camp and had to carry it up Mount Snowdon, in pouring rain and mist. "We had a poor Dutchman who only managed to get half way up and then had to be carried back down again. He'd never climbed anything higher than a dyke."

Battle Camp was tough but John has never forgotten his time in Wales. He enjoyed the experience, even with the non-stop rain. After it, he was dispatched to The Royal Armoured Corp, Officer Cadet Training at Bovington, Dorset, where he trained on the latest tank, the Comet. Bovington was heaven compared to his previous torture at the hands of Sergeant Major Brittain. The junior officers were now considered serious soldiers who knew how to command a troop of tanks in battle.

John finally got his marching orders and set off to join the 11th Hussars. Destination: Detmold, Germany. En-route to join up with his unit, he encountered Vernon Stratton, who became a lifelong-friend. The two men met up at Harwich Docks to board a ship to Cuxhaven, quite a big port between Bremen and Hamburg. Their first orders were to oversee the repatriation of a 1000 German POWs, who didn't need to be guarded because they just longed to go home. "I saw little groups of forlorn looking women waiting for their husbands and boyfriends. I remember being quite moved by it and thinking they have two arms, two legs like us. Vernon thought the same and, years later, we compared notes about it."

Germany had suffered collateral damage and Cuxhaven was a mass of rubble. John and Vernon took the train to Hamburg, now flattened more than London, and spent the night in the SS barracks. All the treasures and valuables had been moved out, but John still remembers the experience: "The Nazis were into all this health through joy, so there were all these muscled men on the walls, angels leaping about, icky looking things."

After Hamburg, John and Vernon boarded the train to Detmold, to the 11th Hussars' base: it was practically a suburb of Bremen, which was flattened, though Detmold was not too bad. They joined their regiment and the first evening in the officers' mess joined in a long-time 11th Hussar's tradition. A silver fox's mask, filled exactly to the brim, took a whole bottle of champagne. Every officer had to drink it and the times were recorded in a book – "I think I did it in about a minute", says John. "And about 15 minutes later, you were really pissed."

British Army of the Rhine (BAOR) army of occupation

It was quite an undertaking for a young man to fit into the most famous regiment in the British army at that time. The 11th Hussars had fired the first shots in the Desert war, were first troops into Tripoli and Tunis, landed at Salerno, Italy, landed D + 1 and been the first armoured car regiment in Normandy. John was somewhat awed by it. "Even my driver had two rows of medals. He was acting lance corporal and didn't want to be anymore than that."

The world felt new, strange, in the aftermath of war, but still buoyed with hope. Europe was rebuilding, streams of army personnel demobbed en mass to take their place in 'Civy Street'. It is hard to imagine now, generations later, what it must have felt like to finally be out from under the cloud of war with its rabid bombs and air raids signalling perhaps imminent destruction.

Post war, Germany was allied occupied and divided into

four zones: Russian, British, American and French. Berlin, which had four sectors, was isolated, because it was in the middle of the Russian zone and the 11th Hussars kept one squadron of armoured cars in Berlin on a rotation basis. With the exodus of experienced soldiers and officers, the colonel had little choice but to use new recruits: young men like John, earnest and willing, not least to show the hated Germans the allied forces were in charge.

The Germans treated the occupying forces sullenly, which hardly mattered to the victorious allies. John was part of the forces who marched the locals down to the cinema to watch a film about concentration camps. Produced by the British and American cinema corporations, many Germans thought the film was faked. If only … However, the would-be producer learnt about cinematic impact.

John's last 3-6 months in the army were somewhat lighter than his earlier days. Acknowledging he was not going to be a regular officer, the colonel gave him the job of running the farm and stables, and he was given a jeep, unheard of for a junior officer. He taught at riding school, open to all ranks, anyone who wanted to learn to ride. And later, he helped organise the horse shows that led to the start of three day eventing in Germany: the 11th Hussars used to challenge the 8th Hussars, and the Inniskilling Dragoons (Skins) all part of The Desert Rats, along with the Third Royal Horse Artillery.

John learnt many things from the army that he uses in business, notably he is a social chameleon, able to mix with all sorts of people from different walks of life. But the most important thing he learnt is how to compromise, a lesson he has never forgotten. This is the story of how he saved the day and turned a potentially life-threatening situation into something more sanguine.

Back then, he recalls, "the Russians were 'our gallant allies' and very friendly and we partied together …". When the Cold War started, Stalin wanted to take over Berlin; he took out the white Russians, the guys who captured Berlin and who John regarded as friends, and replaced them with "Mongolian soldiers that no one could relate to".

John went to Berlin to say goodbye to his friends in C squadron just as the Russians started their blockade and got stuck in Berlin for a week. Finally, in the early hours of the

Deb's delight: Vernon Stratton who John met in the army. On John's left, John's girlfriend at the time, Janet Campbell Jones. [© 2010 John Coates.]

morning after one last party, he tottered to the bus station – buses ran through the Russian zone, a hundred miles or thereabouts. As he was the only officer on site, a transport control officer put him in charge of a convoy of three buses, low, quite smart, and mainly full of women and children all evacuating Berlin. He was handed a brown envelope with his orders in it, and told not to open it until he was out of the sector and into the Russian zone.

There were two soldiers on each bus: "the scruffiest looking soldiers you'd ever see, must have been national service by then", concludes John, "and each soldier had a Lee Enfield rifle and ten rounds of ammunition. We were going to fight the Russians with that, typical British army forward thinking." Luckily, there was a Czech interpreter, who turned out to be helpful. After a lot of "argy-bargy" with the Mongolian people on the sector, Russian zone checkpoint, they set off. All the way to the British zone, and probably on purpose, there were tanks and guns half-hidden: "Stalin wanted Berlin and didn't like the allies being in there at all.

He wanted me to see it and report back that all these weapons were massed around Berlin."

Once in the Russian zone, John opened his brown envelope, which read: "these three buses are part of the British Empire. On no account will you allow armed Russians on board. When you come to the checkpoint into the British zone you will find they want to check passports of all the occupants of the buses, and probably want to send in an armed guard. You will not allow this." John was stunned: "I stopped reading the text and an unimaginable feeling of loneliness came over me – I had no one to turn to".

Sure enough and to the letter of John's orders, at the Russian zone check point a decorated young Russian lieutenant, a little older than John, came up, perfectly polite, and saluted. He had an escort, carrying a "gangster" style Tommy gun with a drum. John was not unduly alarmed at this point, but felt a shudder down his spine when the lieutenant told him he intended to put a man on the bus to check out the occupants, along with an armed guard. If he agreed to this, he was acting directly against his orders: if he didn't, the consequences might be severe, and he had the lives of three busloads of English evacuees in his hands.

Through an interpreter, John explained to the lieutenant he could not do that, and the lieutenant went away, phoned, John likes to think to Moscow, came back and said that was not good enough. The stalemate lasted for hours and John was getting worried because no one knew how serious the Russians were, and there were woefully inadequate arms to guard and protect three busloads – just six men with old fashioned rifles and ten rounds of ammunition each. John didn't even have a pistol.

Then he had a brainwave: he noticed the buses' inside doors closed within a big step. "I thought the British Empire started where the door closed, and if the armed sentry stood on the step it wasn't strictly inside the British Empire." He explained his idea to the lieutenant, who phoned "Moscow" again, John could see him going into a big wooden log cabin, but this time he came back and agreed to his idea. About half an hour later, the three buses and their passengers' drove into the British zone, cheering. "They were all there with binoculars, they had a battalion of infantry on the road ready

15

to come and save us. God knows what they might have done if we had been forcibly detained."

Not long afterwards, John demobbed and flew back to Northolt and home. He was just beginning to unwind from his ordeal when he was ordered back to Germany. "I had to get back into uniform and I flew from Northolt. The airlift had begun, they had stopped the trains and buses, and canals, closed everything to try stranglehold."

John flew to Berlin to explain the bus incident to top brass and had to report to the commander of the Berlin garrison, a brigadier, where he had to account for his actions in one way or another. Then he was allowed to demob. "It was a fine point wasn't it? Where did the British Empire begin? When I said we had reached a stalemate with the Russians and I was responsible for three busloads of women and children, largely British service wives getting out of Berlin, it put a smile on his face. I was quite upset. I thought I should have been given a medal!"

Compromise is now one of John's life maxims and definitely part of the secret of his success. Post army, University had lost its appeal and John wanted to pursue life whole-heartedly. He sometimes wonders about his decision, but, typically, does not dwell on it: "I wouldn't say I never regretted it but I haven't lost sleep over it." Who is to say if he would have become a film producer if he had followed an academic path? He might have ended up a captain of a completely different industry.

3

Early Days at Rank, Far East and Asia

Rank

John was straight out of the army when a media career beckoned. He could have stayed on in the services, but in truth had never entertained the idea and as soon as he finished his three-year stint was ready for out. It was 1948 and he had not long demobbed when a *Times* newspaper ad caught his eye; for people interested in the film industry to join a year-long training scheme with the new J Arthur Rank Organisation. He applied under his family name of Coates, so no favouritism, and following an interview was offered a job.

The film industry was predominantly American at this time, and Rank wanted to change all that by creating an English rival to the big Hollywood set ups. The training scheme gave John a crash course in every aspect of the film business, including a period at Pinewood, the biggest of the Rank studios. "It wasn't about knowing how to edit or shoot, but to learn what putting together a film was about, what it was like to go on the set and see things being shot", he says. "In the end, Rank did achieve what they had set out to do. They did manage to build something comparable to the big American companies like MGM or UA, and Pinewood movies such as *Oliver Twist* and *The Red Shoes* have stood the test of time and mark out a wonderful period in the British film history."

After the relative glamour of the studio, trainees got to grips with the exhibition end of the business via a stint as a trainee

cinema manager. John learnt the ropes in several picture houses in the West End and the suburbs – Rank had a huge cinema circuit, including Odeon and Gaumont. He remembers standing front of house at the Odeon, Leicester Square, donned out in dinner jacket, with his friends jibing him for it. He suffered, "the same embarrassment at Swiss Cottage Odeon, and after that you went to the distribution people".

John specially posed, working at the Rank offices in Lahore. [© 2010 John Coates.]

Rank's Film Distribution was handled by GFD, General Film Distributors, which had absorbed an American company Eagle Lion to handle overseas business. Eventually, the whole thing became Rank Overseas Film Distributors and they bought out the American company. John ended up doing the training scheme at the then Eagle Lion, just as it was changing its name. They were looking for a young person to go to the Far East and act as relief so that branch managers out there since the war could have home leave. John got picked. The training scheme was petering out by then, but he had benefited enormously from it, and so had his social life. "Rank were running a charm school for young actresses at that time – Honour Blackman was amongst them – and us trainees would escort the charm girls to the premiers."

Out to the Far East – Calcutta or bust!

The year was now 1949 and England was fairly depressed, actually a lot more depressed than during the war and rationing was harder, so John was delighted to be sent to the Far East. "It was the hell out of boring old England. And off I went on a Lockheed Constellation, Quantas airways!"

Nothing was set in stone, but a spell of relief duty was typically three years with a three-month holiday at the end of it, which suited John. He flew out, initially to Calcutta, where George Reardon "a nice tubby man" was the Far East supervisor. The flight was non-stop to Cairo with a night at the Heliopolis hotel, a large tourist hotel on the outskirts of the city. Lovely ladies always loom in John's life and here was no exception. He remembers a "very pretty Egyptian girl" sat at the information desk of BAOC – British Overseas Airways Corporation – "the old original". John asked her how he could get into Cairo and the girl, who finished work in 15 minutes, offered him a drive into town. He accepted and a fun night out ensued, which at 21 he thought rather lucky. From there, he went to Karachi, and then to Calcutta, where he was hot-housed, and spent a month or two under his boss's wing, learning what film distribution was about. "I had to sit through endless Indian films, which in those days used to run for hours and hours and were full of songs."

Not long afterwards, he was posted to Batavia, now Jakarta. The Dutch were still there. As if to prove the point, the evening he arrived they shot two people at the checkpoint in front of him. That resonated with John; he had just come out of one war and was now in another. Rank spared no expense on their new recruit and he was put-up in the Des Indes hotel, still Dutch managed, and very international. It was the big colonial hotel and served Rijstaffel, a Javanese dish with a ridiculous number of courses served as a traditional feast for Sunday lunchtime. John can still see the waiters all lined up in a row behind the customer, each with their dish in hand. "It was amazing – you had a big bowl of rice and then they'd come and add all their different dishes.

You had a mountain, and then you'd pass out and go to bed. The whole thing was washed down with beer."

John and Miss Festival Of Britain. 1951, Karachi; she was on a promotional world tour at the time. [© 2010 John Coates.]

John "got about a bit" because the Dutch and the Indonesian rebels had reached a truce and the Indonesian government was being set up. He enjoyed driving to Bandung, the capital, right through the centre of the beautiful island of Java, up over the pass, framed by still smoking volcanoes. A chalet sat a top of the pass, run by a Swiss couple. Surrounded by spectacular scenes, lunch there was something else.

The island sand was black, because it was volcanic, but there were long beaches under the palms and the swimming was gorgeous. There were a few Water Snakes but they avoided people, luckily.

After quite a few months running the branch, John was posted to Singapore, to help-out the manager. The boss in Calcutta gave the call to come back to base. "Don't fly, you've earned a week off" he told John. "Take the British India line, rather a nice boat you'll see. It stops in Penang and sails all the way up the Ganges to Calcutta. Book yourself a first class ticket." John did just that, to discover the only other first class passengers were Seventh Day Adventists, disappointing for a man who likes the odd tipple. He drank alone because his shipmates didn't approve of anything fun.

His usual partying was condemned by "this real busy body daughter, who used to sit in the doorway of the bar and say what God thought of me. Just boozing and a sinner, that's what I was!" But a week later, as they sailed up the Ganges, the girl started to doubt her parents strict views: "She now believed having a glass or two of scotch was not that bad and John wasn't that ungodly. I got stick from her mum and dad and the experience soured my view of water travel for life. I have never been on a cruise since!"

After that, he had a spell in Delhi, where it was "nice, hot, and rained a lot", and then a stint in Bombay, which he enjoyed. Bombay was "dry" and while it was possible to get a doctors certificate to buy liquor, for medicinal purposes, it didn't buy much, so the trick was to know the people who bought it in from Goa a few hundred miles down the coast. A beach, north of Bombay, served as an unconventional liquor store and messengers passed on details of where to pick up the goods. Directions had to be specific "Dimple Haigh bottles in the sand the 33rd boulder on the north side of the lagoon". It took a while to count them all and concealing the stuff afterwards was a bit of an art; people had to get inventive, but the best places were under the boot or back of the car somewhere. The "dryness" was a serious affair, enforced by checkpoints on the run into Bombay. John was too wily to get caught, but lots of people did. A rather nice Muslim lady proved a welcome distraction here; but this was very soon after the partition of India and Pakistan and the stories of the slaughter were dreadful – "millions and millions were killed. Religion again!", says John. The girl was from a rich enough family so they stayed safely in Bombay. She had been to the Sorbonne and was sophisticated. "She wore a two-piece, they weren't really bikinis. It was never a serious affair, only a passing thing."

Back in Calcutta, he was invited to Assam, where one of several snake stories took place.

Snake story –

During his three years in the Far East, John got invited to a tea plantation in Assam, which ran up the North East of India up to the Burmese border. Assam Airways was a bit of a ramshackle affair run by enterprising ex RAF people and consisted of two airplanes, ex RAF Dakotas, where the seats were benches long ways. The one he flew in lacked its loading doors where the jeeps went in and out so the passengers sat facing each other the length of the plane; the locals were in there with their chickens. "After take off, the plane gathered height incredibly slowly and seemed to just manage to fly above the height of the trees as it headed up into the mountains. You looked out of a big hole at the side of the plane. Even now, I sometimes have a funny dream about that", says John.

He was welcomed to the tea plantation where he made a night trip through the Jungle, and saw tigers in the headlights. His guide suggested climbing an enormous tree to observe animals drinking at the waterhole below. Early evening and John had not long been at his vantage point when the guide nudged him and pointed. Sitting on a branch was a monkey with eyes transfixed to the ground. Stock still, it had been there for about 20 minutes when it sprang down to the ground and seized a cobra round the throat. A battle ensued and the two creatures fought for hours. When the cobra squeezed the monkey, the monkey sawed the cobra's head against a rock. "Me and the guide finally climbed down to see what had happened, because it had all gone quiet, and found both animals dead; half the snake's head had been rubbed away and the monkey was choked to death. It was bizarre. Maybe the cobra had killed the wife or girlfriend of the monkey."

Another snake story ...

"While on the subject of snakes, I didn't witness this one, but it was printed in the Lahore Times. I think is worth telling."

In Pakistan during the famous floods of 1951, the five rivers of the Punjab burst their banks. "We drove out of Lahore of an evening to see the ever-threatening floodwaters, along the edge of which was a whole mass of writhing snakes. You have to remember those tributaries are miles across and the villages of the riverbanks were fishing villages. The story goes a whole family got into a boat to escape the floodwaters, but there was no room for their baby so mum put it in a pot to tow behind them. Just as they were pushing off, a cobra leapt into the pot with the baby. A terrified mum let go of the pot and it swirled away in the floodwaters, and later whirled past another village with the baby's head sticking out of the top. A villager ran out to save it, but as they dragged it to shore, the cobra reared up and bit them. Amazingly, the baby was alive and well."

And just one more …

"The only time I was close up to one, I was dining in someone's house in the outskirts of Lahore. Just as I was going to get some beer out of the fridge, I saw a cobra sitting up there. It didn't half give me a fright. That was a proper one and I got quite close. The servants caught it and did it in."

All that "tripping about" was two years and he went to Rangoon somewhere in the middle of it. He found the Rangoon ladies very appealing and remembers going to a nice restaurant, probably also a brothel, "where the girls were seriously attractive and they'd sit on your knee and feed you. The men could go upstairs afterwards if they wanted to, but I was young and shy and didn't. It was a perfectly respectable restaurant, right in the centre of the city."

By now, John felt it was high time he had a holiday and Ceylon, now Sri Lanka, was the perfect place, followed by a sojourn up country to Kandy – the hill resort where the rich went when it got unbearable on the coast. He rode an elephant across the river. They were logging elephants moonlighting as people carriers, but he loved the experience.

After that, it was on to Pakistan, in Lahore where the Rank office was. The English manager, another who had spent his whole grown up life in the Far East, was returning to England for a year and John had to fill in for him. It was to be his last year there so he made the most of it. He liked Pakistan and became a member of the Punjab club, a country club for the elite. On Sunday lunchtime, the Pakistan army used to march up and down with bagpipes, "I think they had them before the Scots did. They were ok at a distance but not my favourite instrument close up."

There was a lot of pomp and circumstance to it all, which John liked. "The Baluchi regiment had pipes and kilts and it was all just like those Korda films, which I loved as a kid." The cavalry regiment added glitz to the parades; they had been in tanks during the war but always had a mounted detachment for these occasions.

The apartment in Lahore was agreeable and in the dry season, the larger part of the year, John slept on the roof. He was permanently brown, a producers tan before even a producer. He was happy to lie in the buff under the stars and, luckily, there were few mosquitoes in the dry period. Dawn broke at about four or five o clock, and by six it was too hot to sleep so he would get up and make his breakfast, though he had a servant who did all his shopping. Most of this period passed without incident, except one balmy night on the roof, the night of the long claws. "The Pakistani people who lived below had a black Scotty dog. One night, asleep, this bloody dog jumped on me, and I had the biggest fright of my life. I felt the claws and fur. It was terrifying."

During his stay in Pakistan, the boss in Calcutta invited John to Kashmir, as part of a group. The plan was to fly to Delhi where they would meet up before flying on to Sirinagar. Kashmir was in the middle of conflicts between India and Pakistan, but enjoying a rare moment of ceasefire. They flew in over the 'Bunny Hole' pass, so called because it had a tunnel, to discover John's boss had booked a lovely houseboat on the lake. He knew the son of the local Marahaja, who came to welcome them and loan a car, an American Ford.

Part of the party was "the honourable somebody somebody, whose husband was part of the civil government and on business elsewhere", says John. She wasn't unattractive and was by far the youngest in the group, other than John, by now a dapper young man of 22. The two of them took full advantage of the Ford and went out on various excursions. On one of their night trips, their car ran out of petrol right on the far side of the lake. The needle didn't show empty so John was surprised when they chugged to a halt; this was dangerous territory teeming with Indian soldiers and anything might have happened. Eventually, an army truck full of Gurkhas came along and offered to help. They had to practically dismantle the car to get to the locked fuel tank, and John remembers them fumbling about in the dark unscrewing the tiny little screws that held it in place. "One blurted out, "oh, fucking hell!" Which seemed ridiculously funny in the circumstances." The Gurkhas eventually refueled the car and sent John and his lady on their way. The couple were quizzed at the houseboat. Where had they been?

Before going back to England after completing his requisite three years, John took one more holiday with some friends and Rachel, "not what you call a serious affair girlfriend but we were pretty fond of each other". She worked for the United States Information Services, and in retrospect John thinks was probably with the CIA. Two other couples and John and Rachel decided to go up the Kaghan Valley on the Pakistani side of Kashmir. "The road had been built so the Pakistan military could access the mountains to fight the Indians, but there was a period of peace and they decided to open the road to tourism – the fishing was excellent."

Anyone traveling up the road had to have a permit, and it was only possible to take a car the first fifty or sixty miles of the route. After that, cars were parked in the village and everyone decanted into army jeeps with a driver. "I had a convertible Morris Minor with the old split screen, which I was very fond of and was the office car." Ever the entrepreneur, John got Nuffield, the Morris people out there, to sponsor his trip if he wrote an article for them, and also got permission from the military to go past the village which no one was supposed to go beyond.

John and Rachel were in the Morris Minor "with all the booze", and the other four had gone up ahead in an American, convertible Sun liner "a big huge floating thing". As dusk fell, the sky split with a thunderstorm so bad it flooded and blocked the road. The road was also closed a mile or two back, so they were stranded with the liquor in what was known as "Safe Tribal Territory". The sky lightened as the storm passed and they heard drums and music up in the hills, quite eerie in the dark in a deserted place. It turned out to be some sort of religious feast. "We had a sleepless night and knocked off one of the bottles of scotch."

The army came and dug them out in the morning, so they caught up with their friends and spent that evening in the

village. Next day, they ascended the mountain road in army jeeps, "we diced with death, some of it was just a cliff face with a drop of 1,000 feet the other side, and the girls spent most of it with their eyes shut". Even so, it was a hell of a holiday. "Before turning back, we drove up a mountain pass of 10 to 12,000 feet. One of the jeep drivers said if they made a short climb on foot, they would be rewarded by a fantastic view of the Hindu Kush mountain range and Nanga Parbat, (the Naked Lady) which stands at 26,000 feet. Of course there was no way we were going to miss that, although breathing at that height was hard work."

That trip finished John's spell of duty in the Far East so he flew back to England, where he had to report to base before taking his three months paid holiday.

His next posting was Spain, and as he had never been there, it seemed a good idea to go and find out what it was all about. He used some of his holiday money to buy MOJ – an aluminum-bodied Austin A 40 sports, 2 plus 2 convertible – so called because of the number plate. He got back together with his old girlfriend, Angela, and discussed going off on the trip, but her parents insisted she take a chaperone.

Morris Minor on the way up the Kaghan Valley. John and his girlfriend got stranded in what was known as Safe Tribal Territory. [© 2010 John Coates.]

26

Angela's best friend and John's next favourite girl was Hannah, so it was agreed she would go along and the three would travel together. Travel allowance was limited to £25.00 foreign currency, but as John had been abroad he was classed as a foreign tourist and not limited to any set amount. Twenty-five pounds does not seem much but was probably enough for a cheap two-week holiday in 1952.

The girls each gave John their money, so that was £50.00, and he took travelers cheques, so with wind in hair and cash jingling in pockets, they headed off for Greater Europe, first stop Madrid. "We drove down western France, stopping off at Arcachon for local oysters and on down to Biarritz, and then next day drove into Spain and through San Sebastien to Burgos for the night. Next morning, they sailed into Madrid and cruised down the Castellana. Hannah spotted the Europa hotel in the Gran Via, complete with roof swimming pool. "It was perfect, safe and cheap and had three stars." Spain was less commercial than now and just on the cusp of taking off. John and his two girls had a whale of a time spending their pesetas and falling in love with the city of Madrid, perhaps a good omen for the days to come.

Some days later, they drove to Valencia, the nearest stretch of Mediterranean coast, and then followed the coastline to Barcelona. Gaudi's stomping ground wasn't much of a hit– it was then just a dowdy, industrial city – so they didn't stay long and instead wended their way up to the Costa Brava, just becoming known partly due to the film *Pandora and the Flying Dutchman*, starring Ava Gardner and filmed at Tossa de Mar. When they arrived, it was hot, dusty and beautiful. That first night they couldn't find a hotel and in the end slept on a beach – it was lovely scorching weather. John and the girls stayed where the filming had taken place and explored the spectacular coastline. They got to know a local fisherman, who one day directed them up the coast for what turned out to be an amazing feast "We found a little track to a secluded beach, and he and his wife came by boat and brought all the ingredients for a paella and cooked it on the shore. We went around the rocks gathering shellfish and things to eat while the fisherman and spouse bought the wine and all the main ingredients." It was the best paella they had ever tasted, and it turned into quiet a soiree on that hot, languid summer's day. Later, towards the end of the afternoon, they heard a car. It was a young Swiss couple in a Kaiser, a large car by European standards but smaller than the American gas-guzzlers. "They were very friendly and helped to finish off all the wine, and joked and laughed along with the rest of us."

That was the last of the stay in Spain. John and co had sampled the best of the country and had a lively time but financial resources were dwindling. If they went to France they could stay gratis with John's oldest brother Michael, so they headed there, always clinging to the coastline.

France

Michael lived in the artist colony of Vieux Cagnes, midway between Nice and Cannes. John and the girls set off, stopping briefly in the Camargue, which proved a disappointment and "really rather scruffy." They drove on through Marseilles, with a brief stop for lunch in Casis, and proceeded along the coast until early evening when the road cut in land across a peninsula. Coming off the hills was "this beautiful bay, which turned out to be St Tropez, in those days just a small fishing port. We drove down to the harbour and settled into the Aioli hotel. It was amazing how we chanced on these places and the Aioli hotel was just the prettiest place ever. We fell in love with St Tropez, so stayed awhile and hit Tahiti beach, the very one the Americans had landed on in the invasion of the South of France."

They could have sojourned longer in St Tropez topping up the tan and generally making merry, but the money was going fast so, sad, they set off for John's brother Michael's place. When they got there, no one was home but a note said "Gone off with a girlfriend to Lake Garda". There was no spare key but the note said to use the window so they made do with that. They stayed for quite a long time, making one extravagant lunch foray at the Beach Hotel in Monte Carlo, where "after lobster and champagne" there were problems with the bill!

By then, it was two months into the holiday and Hannah had to go back to London to work. She knew Rex Harrison's son Noel, so suggested a visit to Portofino, where they had a villa. The plan was to blow the rest of the money in Portofino, just the other side of Genoa a days drive away. Hannah, familiar with the place, suggested a stay at Paraggi, a little beach just short of the actual port. MOJ eventually

MOJ on the Furka Pass.
[© 2010 John Coates.]

got them to Portofino, which turned out to be one of the most beautiful places in the world. "We arrived on a warm romantic moon lit evening, got into the annex of the hotel, dined, and Angela and I swam out into the ocean. It was a blissful, intoxicating evening, and holding on to the anchor chain of a rather smart yacht, we started to make love. Suddenly the lights on the boat came on and shouting was heard ... We swam quietly away."

The next day, there were no Harrisons around, but the trio decided to stay on as long as depleting funds would last and found plenty to keep them occupied. One day, John and the two girls took a pedalo far out into the sea. Angela and John planned to take a swim, while Hannah, not a great swimmer, was happy to stay on the boat and look after her handbag, which held all the money, "a great wad of Italian lira notes". Pedalos in those days were old fashioned with great high wooden seats and they weighed a ton. Once out to sea, John thought he would dive in but as he plunged in the water the pedalo capsized; he surfaced to find the girls and the money

29

in the sea. Hannah was a "real hero" in saving her handbag (with all the money in it) from the bottom of the ocean, but they were still miles from shore. The pedalo was much too heavy to right again, so they had no choice but to sit on it like castaways and thumb a lift. As the strongest swimmers, John and Angela wondered if they should swim and get help when a sleek Italian yacht came alongside, took the girls on board, left John sitting on the top of the upturned craft and towed it all the way back to Perragi harbour – the girls were royally entertained by the Italian crew. Back on terra firma and all three dried off, the money was still sopping wet. Hannah borrowed an iron from the hotel and the three sat ironing the notes to dry them out. Later and somewhat reluctantly, they headed back to Nice and put Hannah on a plane to London. John doesn't think Angela's mother could have cared less about a chaperone really, "it was what would aunt so and so say ... to save all the gossip".

John and Angela stayed only a couple more days in Michael's house before setting off for Zurich where she worked. John planned to drive her back, and on the first evening they arrived on the lake at Annecy and fell in love with it. They found The Belvedere, a rather nice hotel of three or four stars and a concierge. They were allocated two rooms in the annex – it was etiquette then to book two rooms "I think when you were young you were put there ... The concierge separately let us into the two rooms, and then he produced a key from his inside pocket "you'll be wanting this door open too sir", and opened the interconnected door with a flourish. The next day the weather broke into a huge thunderstorm but cleared by the following morning. Angela decided she didn't want to go back to work. She phoned in and said she wasn't at all well, though she "looked amazing" and was going to be late back. We stayed ten days more!"

The hotel garden was on the lakeside, with jetty and diving boards. A smart Chrysler Chris Craft pulled alongside one day and chatted Angela up. "Did we want to try water skiing? Which in those days was more of less unheard of so the skis were great long things adapted from snow skis. The boat wasn't ideal for the sport; it was fast but didn't have the acceleration needed to get the skier quickly up on top of the water. Angela, being a seasoned snow skier, quickly mastered this new sport. John, on the other hand, didn't. It is strange that the lake and town of Annecy have subsequently played an enormous part in his life, having become home to the world's biggest animation festival.

The trip had to come to an end so John drove Angela to Zurich, via the Furka Pass. As they headed into Zurich that evening, down the Bahnhoffstrasse, a car pulled alongside, hooting and waving. Unbelievably, it was the Swiss couple that had appeared two months earlier on the Costa Brava beach. He was a banker and had a lovely apartment overlooking the lake – they were still in their silver Kaiser car. The four had dinner together and Angela went back to work next morning, leaving John at a loose end, but not for long. "I thought I could always call my friend Claudia, who was Lord Ismay's private and personal secretary – Lord Ismay was the boss of Nato in those days. I got the number of the Palais de Chaillot, phoned in the morning and got Claudia. We met and she showed me the sights of Paris, including Carole, a lesbian nightclub, full of the most amazing looking girls – all part of growing up."

It was the summer holiday weekend at the end of August. Trouville, just across the river from Deauville, proved a perfect place to while away time. They found one of those lovely old hotels "where all the servants came and lined up and said goodbye to you". Afterwards, John drove Claudia back to Paris and then returned to England, penniless!

4

Madrid – "We Read Hemingway and Lived Hemingway"

John took up his Madrid post for Rank in autumn, 1952, age 25. He calls it "the most fun time of my life" which culminated in his marriage to the lovely Bettina.

On arrival in Madrid, John rented the previous manager's apartment in the Gaylord Hotel, mentioned in Hemingway's *For Whom The Bell Tolls*. It was quite a centre during the '60s and John had a nice place near The Ritz and The Prado. Two elderly ladies, American expats, befriended him and spoilt him with presents, and enjoyed the occasional glass of sherry on his spacious terrace. Hotel life didn't really suit John, even if there was an excellent restaurant in situ, probably less of a bonus in Madrid where every corner revealed some new culinary temptation. He took an apartment off the Plaza Principeza, somewhere quite central but very different to where he had been living; the plus was a car parking space in the basement and a daily breakfast, sent up to his flat. Madrid was a vibrant intoxicating place. Life didn't come much better for a young man and John made the most of it; not yet tethered by the responsibility of marriage and family, he did what any other red-blooded male would do and partied. Rank paid a monthly salary of £100.00, drawn in pesetas from the bank. As saving at that age wasn't on, he would blow whatever was left over each time on a party, just so he could go back and get the next lot of pesetas. "I got quite popular, not surprisingly."

The rhythm of Spanish life suited the young Brit and he took naturally to the siesta, working in the summer months from 8 until 2, and to the weather, which was baking hot and dry. Typically after work, he'd have an afternoon nap, and then later on head out of town to his favourite nightclub, the Villa Rosa, an all night party house. It was a mad whirl of a place, where they danced mostly Latin America numbers. The Mambo was the dance of the moment, and there were the wildest interpretations going. If the partying went on all night he would breakfast there, have a swim in the pool and go to work. He had a young crowd of umpteen different nationalities in tow, Mexican, Central American and South American, all at Madrid University. It was an amazing life, and with the cost of living so low, easy to live to the full and drink from Bacchus's cup, in this case filled with a cheap red wine called Banda Azul. For victuals, seafood proved plentiful and cheap: Oysters were 9 pesetas for half a dozen, nothing at the time. The fish restaurants were some of the best in the world because the refrigerated trains came from the Mediterranean, the mid Atlantic and the Bay of Biscay each morning. "There was basically every fish you could ever think of, amazing considering the sea was 300 miles away, and Madrid is the geographical centre of Spain", says John.

Madrid had everything, scorching hot sun in summer and in the winter the chance to ski on the Sierra Guardarama, the mountain range to the north. Skiing was rudimentary, no ski lift to speak of, "so you had to herringbone up the slopes", says John, then a novice at the sport. He made his own skiing debut rather unceremoniously when a group drove up the pass to a little alpine hotel, planning to park the cars and ski down. Mumbling he had never been on skis, he stepped on the road, which was solid ice, put on his skis and started sliding backwards. "It seemed like I slid for miles dodging cars coming up the road, who were sliding about, there were no four wheel drives then, and ended up in a huge snow bank."

The girls …

There was a string of pretty ladies, of course. Beatriz, the daughter of a diplomat, was from Central America. She and John became quite friendly but love was thwarted because he was a heretic – not Catholic. Any fraternisation was limited to dates in the early evening: she had to be back home for dinner, people dined late in Spain, but being young and in love they took their chances and often managed to meet late at night by way of the fire escape. They were caught red-handed and she was banished to a country estate where strenuous efforts were made to keep them apart – their letters were intercepted.

Not long afterwards John nursed his broken heart on Pilar, "a Veronica Lake look alike, very un-Spanish, with striking blonde hair seductively covering one eye". Her dad was the managing director of Iberia, Spanish airlines, but she worked in the offices of British European Airways, the old BEA. John was always in and out of there and she sat near where tickets were booked and brought. Then one time he summoned up courage to invite to her to lunch …

Dotchi had royal connections, but wasn't royalty herself. The daughter of the comptroller of the Bulgarian royal household (the Royal family had exiled to Madrid) she was glamorous and fun. When her parents threw a cocktail party for her 21st, they allowed John to organise going to dinner at The Ritz Hotel: "I hasten to add I wasn't paying for it. We had a circular table and I think there were 21 different nationalities around a huge table in the middle of The Ritz Hotel Restaurant. All of the place settings had cards with flowers in the national colours. It was incredibly beautiful."

Madrid did a lot to shape John Coates' life. He met the woman he was to marry there and it is fair to say he honed his business skills there too; his philosophy of lunching started in Madrid. He took over from the previous manager Colin, who told him the secret of doing business in Spain was to never talk business and money in the office. "He said you can welcome them to your office and talk about the weather and God, but that's all. The drill was to go down to the café where the midmorning standard was to order a coffee and cognac, and the minute the cognac was going down, it was ok to discuss business." John has never forgotten that: "I adapted that to lunch and to this day never talk business in the office".

John met his future wife when his secretary, the mainstay

of the Rank office, announced she was going to retire back to England. Faced with finding someone who could take dictation and speak English and Spanish at short notice, John cast about his friends. "There was an inner circle and then there were the fringe elements. In the latter, was a very attractive looking girl who was always mixing with the more sophisticated elements of bull fighting, more specifically the Mexicans, who were sticking two fingers up at the Spaniards at that time and doing rather well", says John. Her name was Bettina and she was someone tall and statuesque, a part time model for the house of Balenciaga, and did a lot of translating for international conferences. She was really attractive but he never thought she would stoop to work for someone as lowly as himself. One day, he summoned up courage and took her out, probably to lunch, and offered her the job. Much to his astonishment, she accepted and became his secretary.

To promote British films in Spain they decided to stage a British film festival in Madrid. The brunt of the organising fell on the two of them; they worked night and day and during that period fell heavily for each other, finally ending

35

up in bed one night having worked until the early hours of the morning. They lived together for the last nine months he was in Madrid, and then John wanted to make an "honest" woman of her. She said yes! "I took her back to England to meet mum, who agreed on the wedding, even though marrying a foreigner wasn't absolutely the ideal."

In the meantime, work was not so hunky dory. There had been a number of disagreements with head office in London, with John Davis, MD of Rank who John considered had lowered the standard of the company's films. "All the glory days of Rank movies, Oliver Twist, Great Expectations, Red Shoes, Hamlet, Lawrence Olivier, Powell and Pressburger and David Lean, came to an end and a whole load of middle of the road movies were made instead." The only British films of note during this period were the excellent Ealing comedies, Man in a White Suite, Passport to Pimlico, Kind Hearts and Coronets, and many more. Sir Michael Balcon ran that operation for Rank and was able to keep his autonomy.

There had been little niggles before John went to Madrid. "It was always a mystery to me why I was sent there, I couldn't speak Spanish and they couldn't speak English." In fact, he was sent to implement a contract: Ranks said they had a bad time in Spain with people not paying, and the general view was they couldn't trust the Spanish. With hindsight, he thought something fishy was going on. They had signed a five-year contract with a company called Europa films, run by Mr Joachim Bernhardt, "a German with a thick neck who looked like a Prussian". John found it difficult working with him, and says of that time, "we had just fought a war with them, and suddenly they were meant to be trustworthy and reliable". Its Board of directors also included the Spanish ambassador in Rome and the Marques de Iglesias, one of the great old aristocrats, so it was an uneasy mix of the posh Spaniards and German fascists.

Soon after his arrived in Madrid, the British Embassy asked John to visit the commercial attaché, who told him that Mr Bernhardt had been the personal friend of Franco and Hermann Goering and helped them acquire the dive bombers used in the Spanish Civil War. It transpired that during the World War, Bernhardt had been head of the political SS in Madrid, and probably had millions of pounds of European art treasures sent out at the end of the war. John relayed all of this information to London, and was ignored, or at least if there was any action taken, he was never aware of it. Next year, he was worried about various goings on and internal people who came and went. Of particular concern was a gentlemen, who he was sure had been a collaborator with Bernhardt. For one reason or another, all sorts of things didn't quite add up.

About this time, he found himself plunged into a real life plot that could easily have been lifted from one of the films he distributed. It starred Mr Otto Skorzeny, no stranger to high drama and a master of daring – most famous for the rescue of the Italian Fascist dictator Benito Mussolini from the mountain prison of Gran Sasso. He had dropped with 90 paratroopers on to the peak and got away in a Storch, a short take off plane. Rescuing Mussolini and generally being a thorn in the side of the allies kept Skorzeny busy, but rumour said he planned to come for Bernhardt and the art treasures. He was charged at Nuremberg, got a minimum sentence, and the morning after he was released John went into the offices of Europa Films and found no Bernhardt – he wasn't coming in that day. A few days later it was clear he had fled to Buenos Aires with £25,000 of Rank's money. What happened to the art treasures? No one knows.

The whole experience soured John's time at Rank. "In a way I was blamed, although they couldn't fire me because I had a fistful of letters telling them what they were doing and had the British Embassy on side." In the end though, he felt he was forever arguing with the UK office, and decided to quit and get married – to the beautiful Bettina.

They married at the British Embassy Chapel with a reception at the Castellana Hotel, and for one night had the bridal suite before pushing off and leaving Madrid for good. Somewhere in the middle of the partying and "carry on", newly wedded John, in full wedding suit, went up to get something from the room. As he stepped into the lift so did his hero, the illustrious Ernest Hemingway, who took him by the lapels and said, "Now young man, do you know what you're doing?" John was flabbergasted. We rarely get to meet our heroes. He is one of the lucky ones.

Just married

The "young marrieds" wanted to do something on their own and decided to start a water ski club. During John's period of notice, he and Bettina had been to Barcelona and had a boat builder build them a speedboat. The couple had studied a little bit about water skiing; yet to take off in Spain, they were sure it would and wanted to help it along. They went to see the Admiral at the Port of Palma and tried to explain the sport. The Admiral, "a dear old boy in his white uniform with all his medals dangling, very Spanish", thought it would be impossible to water ski, and told John, "You can't stand on water like that", but nonetheless couldn't think of a reason why they should not do it.

That might have been the end of the tale, at least as far as film making goes, had it not been for the Spanish Board of Trade. Outboard motors built by Spanish companies were protected but didn't really have the power needed for water skiing; the ones that did were 25 HP American engines, either a Johnson or an Evinrude, and they had to be smuggled in. John and Bettina planned to get one, but when the Spanish government made it a mission to seize or seal every non-Spanish motor they could find around the Mediterranean coast it put the damper on their plans. "We were rather stymied, with a motor boat all smart and shiny and lovely looking and no motor."

Not sure what to do, the young couple talked to their boat builder who located an engine for them, a Johnson 25 HP engine. It was in a boat fair in Barcelona on the American stand so they would have to use cunning to procure it without the Spanish authorities finding out. Somehow, they got into cahoots with the exhibitioners who at the end of the show slipped them the engine, and then filled the box with stones to make up its weight. Even then, they didn't dare to put their craft in the sea in case it was spotted and reported. "The Guardia Civil were everywhere on the coast. You couldn't play about with that. The German who built the boat was helpful and offered to keep both boat and engine free of charge – we had already paid for it."

John knew all the kafuffle would settle if he and Bettina could sit tight until the fuss died down, but they didn't have the money to wait, though they did both consider getting jobs. They had plans to develop a business on the coast

John finally makes an honest woman of Bettina. Here, cutting the cake. [©2010 John Coates.]

where land was dirt cheap, and buy 40 acres of the Costa Brava and to set up a Botel with water skiing. John's mother could have helped financially but disapproved of Franco's politics so refused to help with the money – they could have bought a whole beach with two headlands for £700.00. There was no water or electricity and the coast road was a dirt track, so they would have to spend a bit of money, but it would have made an ideal location for their venture. Finally, with much regret they decided they would go back to London and get proper jobs.

5

How It All Began – Rediffusion and ATV

J ohn and Bettina straggled back to London and rented a
little flat in Nottingham Street, off Marylebone High
Street. It was a tiny place, but laid out well enough so
that it didn't feel cramped. Rather ingeniously, a bath under
the kitchen table saved a lot of space. Settling into London
life, Bettina got quite a well-paid job using her languages
immediately, while John decided the film industry was
finished and the future was TV. The week he arrived back
in London two of the new ITV channels were running ads
in *The Times* for people to join them so he applied for a job.

At the start up of Commercial Television everything was
London; there was no network and only two companies.
Associated Rediffusion (AR) ran programming from
Monday to Friday, and ATV, which programmed the
weekends. John had interviews with both ATV and AR. First
with Lou Grade, boss of ATV weekend Television, famous
for his large cigars and large personality, and next with the
Controller and the Assistant Controller of Programmes of
Associated Rediffusion. The controller was Bill Gillette, a
former VP of programming for CBS who had just arrived
from New York with his glamorous American wife. The
assistant controller, Lloyd Williams, had come from the
BBC. During the interview, one looked at the other and
said, "well we have to start hiring some young people some
time, we might as well start with him". John got hired on
£10.00 a week: "when it got going I earned quite a lot, but

at the start it was small because they weren't going to be on air for almost another year".

The nine-month run up to launch was exciting: Wembley Studios were being built and making TV history. John's duties included interviewing for the many posts that needed to be filled; sifting through applications and even interviewing people for jobs such as vision mixers, not knowing what vision mixers did.

A year later they went on the air: the date was 1955 and the first commercial was Gibbs SR toothpaste. The first transmission is soldered into his memory because everything broke down; finally the outside broadcast used army field telephones (wind up ones) because the others failed, though in the end it all hung together and worked. The company grew rapidly after the first days and soon employed over a thousand people. ATV and AR were in the same building and John's boss would send him upstairs for messages to Lou Grade, who would sit there behind his cigar. "He always called me lad. Come in lad, he'd say."

John worked between Lloyd and Bill Gillette; the latter took John with him when he went to New York to buy programmes, which he loved. They flew on the Boeing President Special with Pan American airways, four engines and propeller driven. It started in Paris where it was loaded with food from Maxims, the whole plane was first class with sleeper bunks; it flew on to London, then Shannon, and then non-stop from Shannon to New York. John remembers, "There was a bar downstairs, a very cosy bar, and dinner was served between London and Shannon, with champagne and caviar. After dinner, people got into their bunks and were woken for breakfast two hours out of New York. A really civilised way to travel."

New York was just how John had imagined it, "full of towering skyscrapers and yellow taxis, like in the movies". As soon as they landed, they were whisked off to another breakfast in The Pierre hotel on the park to see the CBS executives: viewings were arranged for programmes to see which ones to buy or not. They had just checked into the famous Waldorf Hotel, when Bill asked John to get him Walt Disney on the phone. John did a double take, thinking how would they do that, and Bill told him to ring downstairs and reception would get him. In no time at all Mr Disney was on the phone. Surprised at how easy and effortless if had been, John said: "Hang on a moment Mr Disney, I'll get Mr Gillette for you …".

John's UK Television career lasted longer than Bill Gillette's, who he recalls as "debonair, good looking with a very attractive NY socialite wife". They rented a smart house on Eaton Square, with butlers and cooks, but sadly a year later Bill was out on his ear. "ITV lost a lot of money when they first went on air, 4 million pounds in year one. It was quite a serious loss, and he was reckoned to be quite extravagant", explains John. After Gillette's departure, ITV bought in John McMillan to replace him. He was the dead opposite of his predecessor and a former head of department at the BBC. McMillan took John on as his assistant but by then the scene had changed quite a lot: ITV was a network including ABC in the Midlands and Granada in the North. The job was fun, but as the network grew AR made fewer and fewer programmes because ABC and Granada were making programmes as well. The company went from 1200 people and having to find five days a week programming to a much- reduced schedule, which didn't seem to have been well planned.

The reality was the company was now overstaffed and John's job wasn't as busy as it had been. As he had a background in film distribution, John McMillan suggested setting up office to sell ITV programmes around the world. John (Coates) and Eric Major, who would later introduce him to George Dunning, set up the sales office and started selling programmes. John did both for a time, assisting John McMillan and running the sales office.

Not too long afterwards John met George Dunning. He was bored at ITV; the excitement had gone out of it, but he was well paid and would have no doubt progressed up the ranks if he had remained there. Eric Major told him about UPA, an animation studio that was closing down but had a Canadian animation director, George Dunning, wanting to stay on in the UK. Asked if he knew anyone who wanted to run the business side, John was curious so he went to see what "they" were looking for, and arranged to meet George Dunning in a pub just off Grosvenor Square. The meeting went well and on his way home he began to think that working for himself would be much more fun than working

George Dunning. Canadian Animation Director who started TVC with John.
[© 2010 John Coates/ TV Cartoons Ltd.]

for big corporations. No more company politics! He got home and announced he was thinking of quitting ITV to go into animation. Bettina, then pregnant with their first child, looked at him and said, "don't be ridiculous. You know absolutely nothing about it!" Nonetheless, John quit ITV and joined George as business manager of the new company TV Cartoons Ltd. A short time later, 10 November 1956, Bettina gave birth to a daughter, Nicola. It was a time of new beginnings.

He took the baby's arrival in his stride: "I grew up in a social world where the normal life was getting married and having children, so I expected this to flow calmly along", reflects John. "I do think that a strong physical love sometimes makes Dad worry a bit about where his position is 'in bed'. However with the arrival of Nicola I can only remember all the excitement and how, thank God, she turned out to be a jolly little soul. Not much of a hands on father, I just went with the flow and Bettina gave up work and became a full time mum."

6

From Film to Television and the Start of TVC

TVC and George Dunning

TV Cartoons had a better start than most new companies because it could piggyback off the old UPA (United Productions of America), the Disney breakaway group that made numerous programmes, including the famous myopic, Mr Magoo. The London studio had been set up to take advantage of the new commercial TV, but closed probably due to financial problems of its American parent. Nonetheless the English studio was successful and had all the key elements already *in situ* to continue, plus the energy and determination of its former studio director George Dunning to carry on. George was a Canadian so he didn't need a work permit, and was happy to have found a business manager to keep the new venture afloat. Another Canadian, Richard Williams (Roger Rabbit) was also in house.

The company found the backers needed to continue mainly as before, but now with John Coates. A live action commercial company, TV Advertising, TVA, bought 30 per cent, with 70 per cent held by three private individuals, one being a partner in the insurance company, Sedgewick Collins. The other was a city gent, and the third was John's former Rediffusion colleague, Eric Major.

TVC opened on June 5th 1957, and John is proud to say,

TVC LONDON ᴺᴼᵂ ₐₜ 70 CHARLOTTE STREET LONDON W1P 1LR
01·637·4727

TVC moves. A fun way to announce TVC's move to Charlotte Street, where they remained until Grafton Way. [© 2010 TV Cartoons Ltd.]

"I've been there ever since". The new offices were in Dean Street, Soho. Decorators were brought in to splash on a coat of paint, and in the meantime, they hired the ballroom in the Monmouth Hotel in Monmouth Street. The company was then ten or eleven people, including Lola, John's secretary and an ex-UPA girl. TVC, luckily, inherited an

45

ongoing series of TV commercials providing much needed income. John and George were on salaries and didn't own a penny piece of the company, and neither had put any of their own money into it.

Rare photograph of the TVC crew on the roof of their Dean Street premises, taken in 1959. John, in duffle coat, stands in front of George Dunning. [© 2010 TV Cartoons Ltd.]

John took a risk leaving TV to embark on something more precarious, especially as he now had a young family to feed, but he never questioned if he had done the right thing. TVC felt like home to him from day one, and if it all went wrong he had enough work experience to easily find another job. John always liked a challenge and tended to leave things once he had mastered them or lost the spark. Animation was a whole different world and its artistry suited him perfectly. There was also this sense of coming out from his Uncle Arthur's shadow. At TVC, there was no nepotism. He relished the challenge of building something from scratch, and took to his job with zest and enthusiasm.

The new outfit had the advantage of inherited business, ensuring profit from year one. It started with a slate of work and picked up a lot more, with TV and cinema commercials being the mainstay. Seven-second ads did well, such as Lyons Quick Brew Tea where an animated man said, "Does not need one for the pot", a tea making tradition of sorts. There was also the catchy theme tuned Aurora Kia-Ora, a little girl character called Aurora for Kia-Ora orange juice.

Around this time, the company was asked to make industrial films, used to explain complex scientific processes. They did a lot of work for the Central Office of Information and made a full-blown documentary for Ford Motor Company. During these early years, industrial filmmaking became big enough for TVC to form a separate company – Industrial Animated Films ltd, formed in 1959.

The company was doing well, but its board of directors, surprised by this success, started spending ambitiously, including setting up a new studio in Italy – TVC Italia. Some of the London staff left to work in Italy as commercial television had only just started there. "The board was trying to run before it could walk and suddenly in the third year, TVC was not very solvent", says John. The advertising division TVA went bust leaving George and John, who didn't control the money, shocked, but now with the ideal chance to buy the company. Eventually, George's friend Tom Spalding put up a £4,000 guaranteed overdraft at Barclays bank in Pall Mall – Spalding went back to Canada and is still a director but not a shareholder. Using that facility, TVC bought in the shares and set up the new company late 1959, coming into 1960. The shareholdings were: George 51 per cent, John 20 per cent, and Tom 29 per cent. Baker Tilly, who were and still are TVC's accountants, sorted out the deal.

John welcomed the change from employee to partner, though his new status bought added responsibility – the buck stopped with him and George. At home, Bettina gave birth to their second daughter Giulietta, named after the Alfa Romeo sports car. Her big sister Nicola was almost three by then: "Giulietta had a more difficult arrival to this Earth than Nicola and found it harder to grow up", says John. "However the two girls got on well and are best of friends to this day. People said we were the ideal happy family."

At the same time, John wasn't the only Coates making a name for himself; John's sister was fast becoming a successful feature film editor. "In 1962 she won the Oscar for Lawrence of Arabia, but was sadly divorced soon afterwards and moved with her children, two boys and a girl, to Hollywood to pursue her career, where she still resides."

John and George had to ensure TVC remained a viable

47

news and newcomers from TV Cartoons Ltd

APRIL - MAY 1962

"THE EVER CHANGING MOTOR CAR"

Scenes from the latest 11 minute cartoon film produced for the Ford Film Library
Directors: George Dunning & Alan Ball.

Mothers Pride Bread (1×30 sec)
Agency: J. Walter Thompson & Co. Ltd.
Director: Alan Ball.

Time Beer (1×15 sec)
Agency: Domas Advertising Ltd. Dublin.
Director: Alan Ball.

Flinn Dry Cleaning (1×15 sec)
Agency: Scott Turner & Associates Ltd.
Director: George Dunning.

Dutch Butter & Cheese (1×30 sec)
Agency: Notley Advertising Ltd.
Director: Alan Ball.

Hoover Junior (1×60 sec)
Agency: E. W., R&R Ltd.
Director: Jack Stokes.
Live Action: Aspect Productions Ltd.

Melbit Tablets (1×20 sec)
Agency: Young & Rubicam, Frankfurt.
Director: Tony Gearty.

TV CARTOONS LTD. 38 DEAN STREET, LONDON W.1 GERrard 9385

TVC showcases their latest ads and corporate productions in their monthly bulletin, 'News and Newcomers from TVC'. Shown are scenes produced for the Ford Film Library, 'The Ever Changing Motor Car', directed by George Dunning and Alan Ball, and various ads, including Mothers Pride Bread, directed by Alan Ball, Hoover Junior, directed by Jack Stokes, and Finn Dry Cleaning by George Dunning. [© 2010 TV Cartoons Ltd.]

George Dunning and Ron Goodwin, musician.
[© 2010 TV Cartoons Ltd.]

business and both men were determined to trim back any needless expense. They closed down the Italian branch and consolidated the commercial/advertising side and animated documentaries; some had snippets of photo animation or live action, but were mostly animation. These were lucrative films and TVC had some high profile clients, including Ford Motors, COI and the Gas Council – energy films were in demand because animation could capture complicated scientific process. Later, TVC got involved with Royal Dutch Shell, who wanted a corporate image for their international subsidiaries. "We made an unusual, mostly photo animation film, which became the final shape and colouring of the Shell sign today", says John.

Animation also had an application in the Ministry of Defence, especially in ballistics to show how missiles

worked. A small TVC team had signed the Official Secret Act to make films for the War Office and The Admiralty. The TVC cameraman was part of the Official Secrets Act and had to put his rushes into a sealed envelope, which a dispatch rider picked up nightly. "TVC did lots of fairly secret things that were often part of a bigger film. We did the technical bit, the demonstration, but often never saw the final result."

John stands with Steve Wheeler from TV Advertising just before going off on a European sales trip to sell commercials. The car is John's own Sunbeam Rapier, one of his favourites.
[© 2010 TV Cartoons Ltd.]

John was the studio boss, and not involved in the onsite high jinks and shenanigans. He was serious about money, namely ensuring TVC had enough of it to continue business. Jack Stokes, one of TVC's perennial directors (who directed The Beatles series and was one of the animation directors of *Yellow Submarine*; the other was Bob Balser) met John after George Dunning invited him to do commercials for TVC. He was intrigued because he was ex-Disney and George was ex-UPA and remembers John as, "very business like in his grey suit and dark tie, trying to keep order over a lot of loose living animators".

As a boss, John made it his business to know what everyone did and tried to encourage people whenever he could. He was interested in results more than the way they were achieved, and had a philosophy of "well, we employed the best, now let them get on with it". Yet his amiable disposition hid a steely attitude. When it came to business, John was, and still is, nobody's fool. Norman Kauffman, a TVC director and long standing friend who started working there, age 16, says John's nickname was Mr 50 per cent, "because he'd only ever offer people half of what they asked for". Still, for all his canny ways, John had the respect of his peers; he tried to be fair and encouraged staff to improve and advance – many artists happily remember their years at TVC.

While George Dunning was being creative with his pencil and sketch book, John was also being creative, with numbers, working out how to keep the company's operating costs down without sacrificing quality. Each morning, he would come in and catch up on all the productions, find out where everyone was at and what rushes there were to view that morning. He didn't set any delivery targets because animators at TVC were paid by footage, which was ingenious, because the faster they worked the more money they got, but only if the work was up to standard. It was a great way to get quality control. Artists gained nothing by rushing and producing sub-standard work. John's methodology meant he knew exactly what the animation was going to cost, and he quickly earned a reputation for bringing in projects on time and to budget, enhancing the studio's reputation. For all his careful ways, the studio was a happy place to work and had a lively culture of parties and fun. Maverick animators such as Bill Sewell, Rufus Sewell's dad, Jack Stokes, Bob Balser and, of course, George Dunning himself, ensured TVC had a family atmosphere, which appealed to creative types. Jerry Hibbert, who went there in 1970 straight from art school, had a great time at the studio, first as a trainee, and then later as an animator.

7

TVC and The Beatles

Prior to The Beatles, TVC had no particular fame outside of industry circles. George Dunning's film *The Flying Man* won the prestigious Grand Prix at the Annecy Animation Festival in 1962, which had garnered creative acclaim, but not the kind of reputation that would of swung The Beatles series contract their way. Nevertheless, some years later, media frenzy ensued when news leaked out that TVC were to animate The Beatles. That thrust the studio into the spotlight; Beatles mania was in full swing, and England swung with it. The year was 1964 and Harold Wilson was at the helm of Labour Government after over 13 years of Conservative administrations.

It was curious that such a quintessentially English band, four working class Liverpool lads, came to be animated by a UK company paid for with American money. At the time, King Features Syndicate, a division of Hearst Newspapers, handled many famous strip cartoons and animated lots of their well-loved characters. The animation division went through the producer Al Brodax, who had been so wowed with the Fab Four's Shea Stadium performance he had come to England to get the rights to animate them. The Beatles were hesitant about this, but agreed to a TV series on manager Brian Epstein's say so. Brodax was keen to make the show in England because it would be cheaper than using an American studio and he thought a British studio would give it the right flavour. He approached various outfits before settling on TVC, which made the series for three years.

The Beatles animated series was a major hit and ABC's most successful children's programme, but John wasn't a fan, not least because the group didn't have a Liverpool accent. They were voiced by an American actor, who John remembers as "a hypochondriac who appeared for recordings with a briefcase full of pills". The "frightfully British" Lance Percival also did some of the voices and it seemed anything would do, bar a legitimate "Scouse" accent. Epstein refused to allow the series to be broadcast in Britain because of it.

The episodes were filmed in the Dean Street studio, which sat about 40 people. When TVC started work, The Beatles paid an official visit. They were "insanely popular" says John, and the police had to seal off the street at either end. ABC television news pitched camp inside and outside the studio and flew in a top interviewer from New York. It was 1964 and bizarre to see so much activity in a London street when The Beatles arrived in a blacked out limo. The interview was to be conducted around the studio, but they could not begin because Ringo's auntie had not arrived, so they all hung about waiting for her. The proceedings seemed to disturb John Lennon, this was in his pre-Yoko Ono days, who took flight at the cameras and disappeared under a table loaded with small eats and drinks. It was a farcical evening really, but eventually Norman cajoled him out of his hiding place so the evening could continue.

The TVC team was well treated during the series. Most of the episodes were made in the UK, but there were so many that about a dozen were shared between Canada and Australia. Jack Stokes directed the series in London, although the Canadians and Australians directed their own. TVC created the look, design and backgrounds and stories were each built around a song with Ringo and co strumming and drumming. Each episode was six and a half minutes and ran to a strict formula. A two-minute sing along with words played out against semi-animation, which was capped by a thirty-second trailer for the next episode. "The Beatles were churning songs out by the mile at that moment", says John.

The series didn't really inspire John Coates or the crew, but part of the fun was that he and Jack Stokes lived near each other so director and producer would go to Rank Labs and view the first prints. "If the heads fitted the body, we'd ship, but occasionally we'd get Ringo's head on Paul's body, and then we didn't ship", explains John. The work done, they'd drive to London airport to the shippers in the Old Terminal

Line drawings of the 'Fab Four' from the original Beatles series. L-R. George, John, Paul and Ringo. [© 2010 Apple Corp.]

1 to get the material off to New York. Jack hated driving so he always got John to drive, and then criticised his technique. After shipping, they would go to the airport restaurant and polish off a bacon and egg breakfast, allowing John to get home "gently" about lunchtime. His "Saturdays were spent viewing and shipping and breakfast – the only time I'd eat that kind of breakfast", he says.

TVC ended up with nearly 50 of these films, "which for what they are, I suppose are quite good", says John. In fact, the series was hugely successful and put ABC children's television back on the map, but they were of their time and John has no residual interest in them. Even so, they were a bit of a phenomenon back then. Production went through 1964, 65, 66 and the series was a "pretty little contract" for TVC. In the first year, they lost money; the second year they broke even and in the third year did rather well. Aside from one small pilot film for the BBC's Barney the Dog, TVC has never really done series work again, though John has worked as Executive Producer on series for other people.

Canada is My Piano

The Beatles series wasn't the only thing TVC made during that time. One of the most successful and creatively challenging works was the only triple screen cartoon: *Canada is My Piano*, a unique film about the history of Canada. Made for Expo '67 in Montreal, it was part of the Canadian Pavilion's cinema experience. There were five films in all and the Canadian Film Board asked TVC to make the middle film because of George Dunning, the Canadian connection. The film represented the signing of the confederation, which was a seriously touchy thing between the French Canadians and the others. Animation was a softer way to treat it.

The concept belonged to animation director Bill Sewell "He was this mad Australian, dressed as Jesus Christ in a white robe – lovely man", says John. Bill had the idea that the groups of settlers were English, Scottish and French, and to represent each one on an upright piano. Three pianists then played their pianos (each with their flag on the side) in discord, because they couldn't agree with one another. Then, across all three screens, a huge grand piano came up with stars and stripes – America – and threatened to swallow them all. Faced with little alternative, they joined forces against Uncle Sam and started playing in harmony, while at the same time, the image travelled across Canada.

It is not possible to see the film because it needs three interlock projectors, though it was shown in London: TVC persuaded the Odeon, Leicester Square to unbolt their three projectors and focus them on to the CinemaScope screen. The National Film Board of Canada owns the rights but the negative is still in England. The film ends with a close up on each screen of a pair of hands on a keyboard playing the Canadian National Anthem, Oh Canada, and pulling back until there are 6,000 pairs of hands on each screen, which makes 18,000 pairs in total. Ron Goodwin did the music: "he took six or seven grand pianos and laid them on top of each other and the sound is just amazing", says John. It was an emotive piece of film and the Montreal audience was visibly moved. No one could trace and paint six thousand pairs of hands so some clever person had the idea of Letraset to print off the different positions. They were put down on blocks, a hundred at a time. Ingenious. The film took a year to make and ran for five minutes, although as there were three films screened simultaneously actually made 15 minutes of animation. All this coincided with getting ready for *Yellow Submarine* and finishing the series. It was an exciting time for John's daughters who were not yet in the teenage years but still aware of how hip and cool The Beatles were and how lucky they were their father was working with them. It was quite a talking point at school and the girls were the envy of their classmates.

8

The Beatles'
Yellow Submarine

ellow Submarine epitomized the 60s flower power, free love and hippie ideals. Heinz Edelmann's designs woven into the psychedelic tale of good versus bad lightened the collective psyche and contributed to the zeitgeist of the time. A society straitjacketed since the war and the '50s was liberalised with 'the pill' and sexual freedom that went with it. A freeing of attitude that filtered through every aspect of society but particularly manifest in clothing and music. John Coates got swept along with the tide: "girls' mini skirts were so short, they were like belts", he says. *Yellow Submarine* may have bought him kudos from his peers, but on a personal level, it led to the breakdown of his marriage to Bettina, and, professionally, saw TVC nosedive perilously close to bankruptcy. Yet for all that, he has no regrets being involved in something with such a ready-made buzz. It didn't come much cooler than this!

The success of The Beatles' series had inspired Al Brodax to make a feature film, but his vision stopped at an extended version of the TV show, which George and John wouldn't countenance. If they were going to make a film at all, it had to be something far superior, as they explained to him in no uncertain terms.

By the summer of 1967 talk was rife about the film, then just a nebulous notion. The pressure was on to get cameras rolling, but George Dunning felt unhappy because TVC would not be able to do anything worthwhile, yet. The turning point came when Beatles producer George Martin invited the TVC team over to Abbey Road Studios without saying why. John, George and Jack Stokes were asked to sit in the studio control room, mystified why they were there. From their vantage point they could see the 'Fab Four' in the studio, "fiddling about with their girlfriends", as John puts it. He and the rest of the TVC crew didn't realize they were there to listen to a very special event ... Then, at ear-popping decibels, George Martin played the new Beatles LP *Sergeant Pepper* from beginning to end without a break. For Jack, John and George Dunning it was an epiphany! They were all blown away, and slowly but surely George got the idea for the feature out of the music. The Beatles promised TVC the use of any songs on the album, plus they were to write four new songs for the film – massive cachet, and hugely inspiring for TVC.

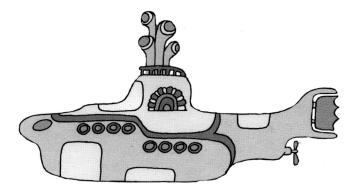

The most iconic image from the film, the Yellow Submarine itself. [© Apple Corp.]

Hearing the music pinpointed the visual style, but it was difficult to capture a 'soundscape' in a look. The search was on but no director of the day, including Jimmy Murakami and Fred Wolf, flown in from America, seemed able to translate the music into image – "all they seemed to be getting was more sophisticated caricatures", says John. In the end, Charlie Jenkins, a former TVC runner who had progressed to be special effects director on the film, discovered the work of art director Heinz Edelmann by fluke. Jenkins was recently married to a German girl and read trendy art magazine, *TWEN*. One day, he bought in a copy of the mag and pointed out the designs to George Dunning. The images were so fresh and different from anything George or John had seen and soon the cutting edge designer was on a London bound plane to talk about the film. TVC briefed him about the concept and he heard the songs of *Sergeant Pepper*. About ten days later, the designs arrived in a brown envelope with a German postmark. John and Alan Ball, one of the staff animators, were spreading the images out on George's desk, when he walked in and said "fantastic", and everyone knew instantly they had found their man.

The discovery of Heinz Edelmann gave George Dunning renewed vigour and suddenly more people were getting involved in the film. Al Brodax was the sticking point because he was reluctant to go for anything more creative than the TV show. John and George eventually won him round by shooting a *Sergeant Pepper* test, using Heinz's characters, which turned out so well it was used in the actual film. They screened the piece at a fancy Mayfair cinema, together with lobster and champagne lunch. Mr Brodax arrived, the lights went down, and TVC looked on nervously while the animated Beatles illuminated the screen. "We had no idea what he would make of it, he didn't know he was going to see anything and bless him, he loved it and said that was the way he thought George should go", says John.

Heinz was to art direct the entire thing, but in the end, the entire thing was on rather a grand scale, so Heinz chose a number two – the late John Cramer who worked for TVC and whom John recalls "as a lovely man and a wonderful talent". He designed the submarine both inside and out.

On the writing side, in the summer of '67, Al Brodax brought an initial treatment penned by an American, Lee Minoff. The writer's attempt was ok but rather Hollywood cutesy, so Al Brodax flew in another American writer, Erich Segal, a professor of Classics at Yale, who later wrote *Love Story*, and installed him in the Dorchester Hotel. Heinz Edelmann and the film's creative team began working with him and were able over long periods of time to produce an acceptable script, although in fact Liverpool poet Roger McGough wrote a lot of the wittier material. He was paid a modest fee but didn't get a credit, which John calls "an absolute disgrace". Al also flew in Abe Goodman as their production supervisor. In the autumn, as production began, Bettina invited the Americans for a dinner party and did

John proud by serving grouse; the Americans had never eaten it.

There never was a full script or storyboard for the film, but somehow the thing evolved. The essential theme of odyssey historically well mined in the works of Jules Verne, James Joyce and even Herman Melville in Moby Dick, was kicked into the 1960s and spun on its head for a new generation. This particular journey of Old Fred, a sailor who travels in a yellow submarine to get help against the Blue Meanies, proffered a rich backdrop for The Beatles mod tones. Rather than being the long-nurtured creative vision of one man, the film was, said Edelmann himself "white noise" a patchwork of different talents and artists with no one person responsible for all.

The band could never make recording sessions at the same time, so actors voiced The Beatles. Variety magazine was unaware of this and when they reviewed the film said their voices were all instantly recognizable. The TVC team really wanted to use the "lads" own voices and kept postponing recording sessions to that end, but eventually they gave up trying and used worthy "sound-alikes". The Beatles didn't like their own 'voices' in the film, although they liked each other's. George Harrison was the trickiest to get right, and is actually played by Peter Batten, not an actor at all, who George Dunning discovered in a pub when he heard a Liverpool accent that was spot on for the film. Jack Stokes went over to the owner and offered him a voice test, and that is how they got their George Harrison. He didn't seem to do a job and hung around the studio, chatting up all the trace and paint girls, and fell for the assistant editor, Jo, who took him in. Months later when the film was almost complete, John remembers she arrived at work in tears. "It's Peter. He was an army deserter. The Military Police came in and took him away." Paul Angelis, who voiced Ringo, recorded the rest of Peter's part, and did it very well.

In the autumn of '67 the storyline began to take place and TVC started to film quite long sections of story and link the songs together. There were two animation teams, one under Jack and one under Bob Balser, who had come to George's attention when his animated short, The Hat, won the jury award at Annecy. Storyboarding was taking place as *Yellow Submarine* was being written; and within a few months TVC had rented sizeable additional premises in Soho Square and had well over 100 people working there. A film that still had no finished script or storyboard and was really put together bit by bit was something of a miraculous achievement. "How can you make a picture when you don't know what the story is?", asks John. The crew grew from a small team to 209, and TVC had to build desks, find cutting rooms and buy all the equipment needed for a large-scale production. A skeleton-staff managed everything, which suited John, never a fan of over administration.

They plunged into it, and by January/February had hired every tracer and painter in London, and there was no way they could meet the deadline: the premiere was July 17th at the London Pavilion Cinema. Luckily, George had the idea to enlist the help of London art students. A few phone calls around the local art schools did the job. The students, all paid the "proper rate", were bussed in for the evening and would work through to 4 or 5 in the morning. Mid shift, they got "meals on wheels", bangers and mash. "I think they had terrific fun. All they needed to do was to be able to paint accurately, even under the influence of 'pot', which was readily available."

60

The team worked around the clock but at least they were catching up.

John remembers an extract from his journal: "I never seem to go to bed". It was an intense period for him both professionally and personally. He was falling in love with Chris, the woman he eventually left his wife Bettina for, married, and still lives with to this day. "I used to wait in reception in the morning for her to come in. I used to find some excuse to gossip in the reception area – she'd step out of the lift in her mini and boots."

John's domestic situation was to come to a head, eventually, but meanwhile he had a film to finish so he focused on that and kept the lid on his affair. Around this time, there were ripples of problems to come. TVC's big model of the *Yellow Submarine* went missing. Normally it sat next to the TVC receptionist, "an amazing Norwegian blonde lady who Jack fancied", says John. "Luckily she was well built or he would have squeezed her to death." Not long afterwards, about April, Brodax said King Features were not paying the staff because the film was behind schedule, which John says was tenuous as what film is ever dead on time? Given Brodax's decision, he explained that TVC didn't have the resources to pay the crew so production was going to have to stop, and then the troubles really started.

George and John had a meeting; at that point, they had two of the seven reels "negative cut" at Rank Labs and until delivery of the film everything was in TVC's name. They phoned the night supervisor, drove down to Rank Labs, arriving there a bit after midnight, and took delivery of the negs. Next morning, they took them into George's bank, the Bank of Montreal. "It's the only time I've seen those big steel bank doors", and put them into the vault, where they couldn't be removed without the signatures of both men. There were all sorts of wild stories that George had hidden them in the bottom of his garden but the truth was far less dramatic, though still very effective.

The two men had mini vans for their wives, because there was no purchase tax on them. That night they decided with the wives and their vans to go round to Knightway House to take the artwork that matched the negatives so they could not be re-shot. Maggie Geddes, a girl John fancied, was in charge of the nightshift. He explained to her that everyone

John Coates stands behind Beatles drummer, Ringo Starr, for the live action shoot at the end of the film. [© 2010 TV Cartoons Ltd./ John Coates.]

had to leave the premises there and then, but could not say why. Maggie was distraught; she was overloaded with work and didn't want to go anywhere until she had scenes ready for camera the next day. John reassured her not to worry and told her to go. She burst into tears; the team was under that much pressure. When the girls had gone, George, John and wives carried the boxes that matched the two reels, loaded them into the two mini vans, and hid them in the basement of George's house in Pembroke Square. By then it was half past four or five and getting light, and they decided to go for eggs and bacon at the Londonderry Hotel. No one knew anything was amiss and it was ages before the boxes were missed.

Yellow Submarine came to a standstill, with the papers saying it was a strike, supported by the union, ACTT (Association of Cinema and Television Technicians). Jack Stokes carried on story boarding regardless as he knew if they fell behind they would have a hard job to catch up when the mess was sorted out. Having reached an impasse, John and George were advised to see counsel, who suggested TVC's only way out was to say they could not pay the staff and therefore had no choice but to put the studio into voluntary liquidation. After that meeting, they staggered out in to Lincoln's Inn square in a state of shock: their "lovely company" might have to close, but bearing in mind the cost of seeing counsel they thought it would be best to take his advice!

The lawyers for TVC and King Features gathered for a showdown, embarrassing as King Features' UK legal team also acted for John's mum. TVC's lawyer reiterated what counsel had suggested: if King Features didn't continue the payroll, production would be brought to an end and TVC closed. Just in case they were unsure about English law, the home team lawyers politely spelt it out: the unfinished *Yellow Submarine* would be taken as TVC's only major asset, and it could be three or four years before the legal side was sorted out. The Americans had not expected such a turn of events and the news struck Al Brodax like a gong. "While he composed himself, the lawyers gathered up their papers and briefcases, and said, we don't think we should continue this meeting." It broke up. Al Brodax had little choice after that but to immediately start to fund the production, but that put a chasm between the two camps and they never spoke again. Throughout the rest of the film, the US and UK teams were very separate. "We (TVC) viewed the answer print at Rank Labs in the morning and they in the afternoon. And though we were both at the premiere we were carefully not seated together or at the party afterwards", says John.

The premiere is engraved on John's heart: "17 July 1968, I've never seen anything like it ...". Held at the old London Pavilion, Piccadilly Circus, it was fancy dress, on the theme of *Yellow Submarine*. Bettina and John went to the premiere as a couple, though they were already on the rocks so it was really about keeping up appearances. Dennis Abey, the live action director who shot the real scene of The Beatles at the end of the film, gave them a lift in his yellow Morgan, but could not get near to the Pavilion because the whole of

Piccadilly Circus was blocked off – in those days you could leave a car on the pavement. The Party afterwards was at the Yellow Submarine nightclub, specially opened at the Lancaster hotel in Bayswater, and John to this day cannot remember getting home: "I think we stayed up all night". Jack Stokes recalls the chaos of the night, worst for him, as he had to set up the screening then dash over to the premiere.

The whole thing had been exhausting, says John. "George (Dunning) and I didn't know whether we'd made something good or not. It seemed so frenetic, but at the end everyone said they enjoyed it – and that's what it's all about." In retrospect, he thinks The Beatles never committed much, not even to the voices. "Funny enough, they all thought the voiceovers were great, except for their own." In recent history, with the re-release, George and Ringo said they really loved the film. John (Lennon) said in his statement that he liked it, particularly the design, but accused TVC of plagiarism. "Totally untrue!", counters John. Paul McCartney had envisioned more of a children's film and said of *Yellow Submarine*, in his book, *Many Years from Now* (co-authored by Barry Miles): "and there's a nice twilight zone just as you're drifting into sleep ... I remember thinking that a children's song would be quite a good idea and I thought of images, and the color yellow came to me, and a submarine came to me, and I thought, 'Well, that's kind of nice, like a toy, very childish yellow submarine'."

Al Brodax and John finally met again when MGM UA made a surround sound edition of the film, and polished up any shaky bits in the original. The new version premiered and the old crew was invited to a screening at Philharmonic Court, Liverpool. Heinz Edelmann and Bob Balser came over and Al Brodax got to hear about it and appeared out of the blue. Geoffrey Hughes, the actor who voiced Ringo was there and said, "I thought Al Brodax was dead", just as he walked in. "He must have felt a bit out of place, although the TVC people were perfectly nice to him", says John. "It was strange to meet face to face again after all those years. George would have probably turned in his grave, but I'm not one to bear grudges."

On the credits John is simply listed as production supervisor, though he was more of the real producer than

Al Brodax, who has the producer credit, but was more of an executive producer who did all the major deals with The Beatles, George Martin and United Artists. Despite the critical acclaim of the film, TVC didn't make a penny from it: they made it as a studio for hire and never took a percentage of the film's gross. Unfortunately, *Yellow Submarine* went over-budget and they lost money making it. King Features gave them their last cheque when the film got final approval and that was that.

"How the film ever got made is a bloody miracle", says John. It was an amazing stroke of luck that brought together all that talent and the crew forged a special bond that still holds today. A debt is owed to art director Heinz Edelmann, a man of immense determination, charm and gentle ways. Jack Stokes, animation director, with not such gentle ways – George had a special door built to Jack's office, which was covered in rubber and spring loaded both ways so he wouldn't kick the walls down! He is still one of my best friends. Bob Balser, animation director, whose devotion and loyalty to the production and TVC has lived on, and who also remains a really good friend. Ellen Hall, company secretary to TVC, who, stood like the rock of Gibraltar in the face of King Features skullduggery, and me asking for five pounds from petty cash to buy a round of drinks for the workers in the Dog and Duck, says John. And who could forget Norman Kauffman, who came to TVC age 16 and grew up as general dogs body on *Yellow Submarine* and is now co-director of the company."

Yellow Submarine was full on and all the team had to work, hard. Nearing the end of it all, John showed his support for Norman when he gave him permission to take his honeymoon, against the wishes of Al Brodax. John advised him: "Norman, hopefully you'll only have one honeymoon in your life, so for heaven's sake go on it!" which is just what happened in the end. Norman was grateful for John's support at that crucial time and also for his salary, which was then a fortune, £25.00 a week, now probably equivalent to £50,000 a year.

No summing up of the history of *Yellow Submarine* is complete without John's "very special mention" of George Dunning, overall director and the late co-owner of TVC. "George was a very gentle man and it says much for his courage that the look and integrity of the film is as a result of his determination to do something a whole lot more adventurous than The Beatles' series that had preceded it. In spite of his failing health, he stayed hands on with the whole production to the bitter end." It says a lot for the *bonhomie* of the whole TVC crew that many years later George Martin, music director, said to John that *Yellow Submarine* was "the happiest film he'd ever worked on".

There is a misconception that the film was made in America. An article in *Time* Magazine, which is owned by Hearst Newspapers who in turn owned King Features, about the *Yellow Submarine* mentions Canadian director George Dunning and German art director, Heinz Edelmann, and otherwise infers it's an American Production. There was no mention it was made in London! A final curiosity! It became the Queen of England's favourite film.

9

Endings and Beginnings ...

With *Yellow Submarine* wrapped up and delivered and the worst of the financial problems solved, John was falling more in love with Chris, spending increasing amounts of time with her, finding excuses to get home late, and fulfilling all the marriage break-up clichés … .

The affair had started when John was working insane hours on the film as well as deal with the stress of TVC's near bankruptcy. All this took a toll and the normal calm and unflappable John had resorted to taking sleeping pills for the first time in his life. *Yellow Submarine* was nearly at the end of production and most of the main team was located at TVC's new premises in Soho square. Chris, together with another girl, Annie, had painted on Lucy in the sky with diamonds and were two of the few people left at TVC's old offices ... John would go up on Sundays to talk to the crew, with the ulterior motive of chatting up Chris who he was already falling for. One Sunday, Annie was unwell so Chris was on her own … John kissed her … It was April 1968.

Their romance continued a pace and John quickly realised he was heavily involved and couldn't just walk away. He confessed his affair to Bettina sometime later that year, sitting on a bank at the top of the lawn at Maidenhead Way, the family home. He tried his best to find a way through the emotional tangles and hoping to find some clarity, for a few months spent the weekends with his family and the weekdays with Chris. It is a period that his daughter

Giulietta for the most part blocked out. For his eldest daughter Nicola it was more difficult as Bettina had confided in her beforehand that her father had met someone else. Still, hoping to salvage her marriage, Bettina put up with John vacillating between her and the 'other woman' for several months, even though she knew her marriage was coming to an end. Eventually, her patience gone, she told him it was time to make up his mind. And John, as he puts it, "followed where his heart led him at the time and stayed with Chris".

It was Christmas of 1969 (the year Armstrong walked on the moon!) going into 1970 when he eventually told his daughters what was happening, although Nicola knew pretty much all of it already at this point. The whole thing was much more of a shock to Giulietta who remembers their last Christmas as a family. "Mum and dad were sitting side by side on a little sofa, and mum had her arms wrapped around herself. Dad put his arm around her and said something caring, and she pushed him away", says Giulietta. "I was so shocked. I'd never witnessed hostility between mum and dad before. I looked over at Nicola for reference and was surprised she didn't seem that shocked. It wasn't until later I found out what was going on, that mum had confided in her."

John eventually told his young daughters on Boxing Day, after Bettina had told him to get on with it. Giulietta remembers he took her and Nicola into the kitchen, sat them down and said, "your father has done a terrible thing …". She immediately panicked, thinking he'd done something so dreadful he would be sent off to prison. That's when John confessed he'd fallen in love with another woman. The next day he was gone. Nicola wasn't so shocked when he left, but it was just incredibly sudden for Giulietta. "I remember in the playroom we had a tape recorder, one of those 1970s tape recorders. And we'd taped *Let It Be* that Christmas and a few other things. And I remember the emptiness now."

With John gone, for the girls it was all about their mum then; they did their best to help her pick up the pieces of her life but she could not and cried every night. Doing her best to cheer her up, Giulietta would go downstairs and dance ballet steps for her. Blocking out the pain in the way children do,

John and Bettina's house, Heathside at Littlewick Green, near Maidenhead. [© 2010 John Coates.]

she doesn't remember any of the run up to John's leaving other than a lot of fun and excitement about The Beatles' film and the general hubbub of lots of parties and people coming to the house. Nicola remembers it differently because she was older, a teenager by then.

John's friends were shocked by the marriage breakdown of what they considered a sturdy couple. Married for 14 years when he finally left the family home, he says now that his wife had started drinking heavily before he left, and the marriage was already on the rocks. Bettina had suffered badly from depression and drank to feel better. John felt sad when he left but relieved he had finally made up his mind. He has felt guilty ever since. "I always think it's the only bad thing I ever did because my wife went down hill very quickly. She took to drinking a lot more and died of sclerosis of the liver." She never recovered from his leaving her, and John still feels responsible for that in a way, but at the same time if he was honest says he probably would not change anything, perhaps he knew Bettina would unravel at some point. The girls don't judge their father and reason that a lot of people experience breakups but they get through it. Their mother never did; she had a damaged childhood. She was always fragile and when something like this happened, she could not cope.

John lived with Chris, but tried as best he could to balance his old family with the new – to ensure he kept contact with his daughters and as cordial a relationship as possible with Bettina. The fall out of his split from Bettina damaged his relationship with his daughters, though it is all water under the bridge now. John understands: "I think they thought Chris was 'that' woman and dad was iffy. We long since made it up in a way, but I don't blame them. Their mum went to pieces and wasn't a good mum any longer. They had a rotten growing up. They went to fairly posh schools, which I helped pay for, but I can't say they had much of a happy childhood. We'd meet up for birthdays and Christmas kind of thing. They used to come down to the house, and we'd have barbecues in the garden in the summer. But they fizzled out, I don't know why."

With his personal life in a state of flux, John's business life was also messy. For all its critical and box office success *Yellow Submarine* had actually damaged TVC. They had worked day and night during the latter stages of the film, so much so that from the end of 1967 they weren't really able to fit in commercials, their normal income, because they were so busy with the crazy delivery date – 11 months for a ninety-minute film! They had to say no to their best clients and that harmed them a lot. Getting back into commercials was hard, but they were desperate to do so because they were so impoverished at the end of the film – they were insolvent and their accountants told them to close down. John and George both breathed a sigh of relief when work came in from unexpected quarters, such as the animated credits for one of the Inspector Clouseau films, and by some miracle they were able to stay afloat.

Still, this was a very bad time in TVC's history. On one hand they were famous, but on the other poverty struck. It was a curious place to be. In the summer of 1968, John went cap in hand as he puts it to "persuade people from bankrupting us". Their two major creditors were Rank Film Laboratories and the Inland Revenue; they had not been able to pay their PAYE for a year. Rank trusted them; after all he was family, so that was ok, even though they were paying them off until years afterwards. The Inland Revenue was a different matter; they also had the power to close TVC down on the spot and John had to plead to save the company. He went right to the top and saw the senior lady of the Inland Revenue who was based in Holborn. The appointment was for 4 o'clock in the afternoon. He arrived just as afternoon tea was being wheeled in and remembers the lady official said, "ahaa, Mr Coates, I'm sure you'll join me in a cup of tea", which was served in posh, fine china. John proposed that as TVC had laid-off most of their staff, including his girlfriend Chris, they were going to be paying a much-reduced PAYE, so they could pay back the money owing in 12 monthly installments. He was "royally torn off a strip or two", but much to John's amazement the senior tax lady agreed to his request. TVC didn't do badly in the end: "The money was paid back in 13 months instead of 12. George and I stopped paying ourselves and drew ten pounds a week from petty cash. I could finally sleep." John was 41 at the time.

TVC survived to live another day and by 1969 they were out of the danger zone. John was able to pay himself a modest salary important as he had to pay his daughters school fees, but the company still suffered financially. *Yellow Submarine* was a huge success, but King Features were not very sympathetic to TVC's plight.

After the film, TVC got back into commercials again and animated documentaries, a market dwindling back then but now totally disappeared. During the ten year period until George died they also did several TV and film projects. One of the best was for Children's Television Workshop, who had set off to make two TV one-hour specials of *The Lion, the Witch and the Wardrobe*. CTW gave the job to Bill Melendez, but he was too busy on *Peanuts* so he handed the whole film to European studios, which was his son Steve in London, Bob Balser in Barcelona and TVC. John liked Bill Melendez and TVC got on famously with him. "At the end of the production, he was generous and appreciative – he sent a cheque for $40,000 to cover TVC's modest extra expenses." The two specials were shown prime time on CBS and were remarkably successful, John winning a producer's

Nicola, John's eldest daughter.
[© 2010 John Coates.]

Emmy, which he recalls was "much to George's astonishment".

The work for CBS took about a year or so, after which TVC got involved in creating two of the sequences in the animated feature *Heavy Metal*, based on the eponymous comic.

Heavy Metal was for Ivan Reitman, a Canadian, who has made a lot of features over the years, including Ghost Busters. John remembers that unlike Bill Melendez, Ivan was a little thrifty when it came to giving out extra payments. "All the makers of the stories queued to see what extra money they would get for doing things that were above and beyond – TVC always did things that were above and beyond. All we got was $3,000 extra. Reitman said that was very generous."

Still, it was quite an elaborate feature and kept the company busy. TVC did the opening: Jimmy Murakami directed the part where a Chevrolet sports car fell through space. "He got the tallest crane in America, and a cult Corvette car, heavily insured, was pulled up and dropped", remembers John. The other sequence was called Den and was handled outside TVC by Jerry Hibbert as producer, with Jack Stokes directing. "A boy playing with computers presses the wrong button and shoots out to space. He ends up on this planet run by a large-titted queen, and finds he has become a super-hero. Jerry and Jack had the time of their lives", says John, who regards Jerry as both a good friend and colleague: "He really grew up with us and went on to form his own successful studio, Hibbert Ralph, and continues as a fun lunch partner to this day."

Jerry, for his part, speaks highly of John and how he influenced his life. "First of all John was my employer, he gave me my first job, then he has kind of overseen my career really. I owe him everything, him and George really." More generally, he credits John with "laying down a template for how to conduct yourself in a business that is a lovely business to be in". Years later, when he set up his own studio, HRA, Jerry tried to bring in the same fun attitudes to working life that he relished as a trainee at TVC years ago. "I like to think that some 25 years or so later we've copied the pattern."

Not that it was all halcyon days at TVC: getting the company back on track after *Yellow Submarine* was a slog, but while John's work life was up and down, away from work he couldn't have been happier. He and Chris were in love and the two travelled as much as possible, taking longer trips when time allowed and shorter trips when it didn't. Chris accompanied John often as possible, especially to glamorous events like the Cannes advertising festival, where she loved to be the belle of the ball in some 'wow' of a dress. It was on one of these trips that led John to his beloved Provence, where he now has a house.

His love of the area dates back to 1972 when he and Chris were attending the Advertising Film Festival in Cannes. One afternoon, a little bored with the festival, the lovebirds decided to escape from it all and head up into the hills to find somewhere cool and nice to have dinner. They drove quite a long distance, up the autoroute, up through Draguinan, and discovered a whole area of military, France's biggest training area. Dodging the tanks, they managed to cross over the whole battlefield, or so it seemed to John. At the top end of the Gorge du Verdon, they decided to follow the route with a mind to stopping in the village of Aguine and having dinner at a restaurant called the Altitude, the highest restaurant in the area. Towards the end of the gorge as they started to descend into the setting sun, they were amazed to see a large expanse of water, the Lac de Sainte Croix, not yet on the map back then – it was a whole valley that had been flooded as a reservoir for Toulon. Chris wasn't a great map reader and John was sure she had taken them off track, but they carried on regardless and descended down through the village of Aguine to Les Salles, where there was a big building site and a board saying this was the village of Les Salles buried at the bottom of the lake but was being rebuilt. It was about 7 or 8 o'clock, the sun was just setting, and they decided to go back up to Aguine and dine at the Altitude restaurant, where they had a great dinner. They found the whole area fascinating and beautiful in many ways. They trundled back in the middle of the night to Cannes to face the festival, but had both been really impressed with the area and over the years came back for many holidays.

During the latter period with George Dunning and TVC, John worked hard and hardly had any long holidays, though he made sure to skip off to Provence as often as he could. Around 1978, when things were better financially and at the end of one of the big projects, John decided to (a) treat himself to a new Triumph Stag and (b) a month off. George wasn't thrilled; he thought it was frivolous of John to just go off like that, but John felt he deserved it and wasn't about to discuss it beyond that.

John and Chris set off in style in his sparkling new Triumph

Stag, a sleek stylish car, roomy and sporty at the same time. The plan was to drive down the middle of Europe to Yugoslavia, down the length of Yugoslavia into Greece, down to Athens and across the other side and then take the ferry to Corfu and then to Brindisi. After that, the plan was to drive to Rome and stay with friends, then journey through Italy to the south of France and up the Rhone valley back to England. As usual, John didn't book anything, except to get across the channel, and set off. He and Chris never actually went to Athens; they crossed Greece somewhere in the middle, but otherwise followed the plan close enough.

The trip was peppered with amusing incidents and trying to deal with the language barrier bought all the usual cross-cultural misunderstandings. Yugoslavia was then at the height of communism and was rather strange. John, a great foodie, always likes to try local cuisine. One evening, he and Chris drove up to a pretty chateau converted into a hotel and restaurant. Used to being heeded, John was surprised when none of the staff took notice of him or Chris. Regardless, they went to the restaurant and sat at a table, where they could see the waiters nearby just sitting on a wall and dangling their legs as though they had all the time in the world. Finally, one of them sauntered over and spoke to them. They eventually had their meal, which turned out to be satisfactory, but John was disgruntled by the surly service they had to put up with. Everywhere they went in the former Yugoslavia they had the same treatment, though they never got used to being treated in such an off-handed fashion. John wonders if it was because the Stag was a fairly flash looking car and the locals thought 'capitalists'. But for sure, he wasn't much taken with Yugoslavia.

Next stop was Greece. They arrived in Corfu on a tank landing craft, which reminded John of his old army days. Not knowing where to go, it was evening, they decided to stay in the main town for the night and look around the island the next day, which they did. They were on quite a tight budget but found an ideal little hotel that was incredibly cheap, sitting to the south of Corfu town, right by the edge of the sea ... "Literally, you had dinner sitting with the water actually lapping at the edge of the terrace". Anyway, they arrived, checked in and had a swim. The weather was gorgeous, so there didn't seem any need to put the hood up on the car. The next morning, they came down to find the car was covered in turkeys; they were sitting all over it and had shat all over the interior of his lovely new shining car and scratched the paintwork. Massive disaster. They cleaned the car up in the end and remembered to put the hood up at night. Later, they found out there was turkey farm just along the beach and they had all escaped.

For all its romanticism, the food wasn't that great in Greece, but John wised up and found the trick to good eating there was to avoid smart upmarket places with flashing neon and use the local provincial places, where the food was always delicious.

Rome was the next leg of the trip and there they had a much better time, eating and drinking in the atmosphere, and the romance. They didn't stop off at Portofino this time, where John had holidayed with the two girls many years previously, and instead, as they both drove, chose to drive all night. The car did well considering the miles it had clocked up, especially since Stags had bit of a reputation for breaking down, although John had no problems with any of his – he eventually had three.

The Stag had not yet been seen in Italy so everywhere they went people wanted to check the oil just as an excuse to nosy under the hood. It wasn't an out and out sports car at all, more of a grand tourer really, but it could still travel, and could even hold its own against 'fast' cars. Joining the autoroute near Valence in the Rhone valley: "a Porsche went past at high speed, this was before speed limits, and it was being trailed by a Ferrari. Chris challenged me to catch up the two cars, so I put my foot down. We didn't pass them but we did trail them, at about 120mph, which was probably near the maximum in those days."

At the end of the summer holiday, John made a trip to drop off his daughters, now young women age 20 and 18, at the university of Aix en Provence. Giulietta was on the back seat with the luggage that would not fit in the boot. It was raining heavily when they set off for Dover to catch the hovercraft. They put down the electric windows (the Stag was one of the first British cars to have them) to show their passports, but then John's window jammed, and the rain was getting heavier! They queued to get on the hovercraft, luckily they queued fairly quickly, but when they got to France it was midday so garages were closed for lunch.

The only sensible thing to do was to have lunch as well, but they needed to be somewhere where they could keep an eye on the car. John found a simple restaurant on the side of the road, which luckily had one parking space. He went to pull into it and a man in a little 'Citroen Deux Cheveux' nipped in before him. Livid, John blasted "Oh, fucking hell", and slammed his fist on the centre console. The window shot up! Not needing a garage after all, they drove on south and stayed the night close by. On arrival in Aix, he stayed a day or two to see the girls settled in; they were at Aix University on a one-year language course. Both girls stayed on after the course, and lived in France for quite some time.

On his return, John got back into the swing of things at TVC, who were still busy with commercials and industrial animated films. Still, the studio owned nothing it helped produce and had no rights in anything other than its art films. John thought there had to be a better way to secure TVC's future in a very competitive time and was by then leaning towards IP (Intellectual Property) development. He would have discussed his niggles and thoughts with George, but George's health was failing and that changed things. George Dunning died in the February of 1979. It was a sad time for John who had lost his friend and his business partner, but at the same time it also heralded a new era in TVC's history.

10

Post George – A New Era ...

J ohn closed his office door when George died. Something was on his mind. "Only if I was firing somebody
was the door closed so the whole studio couldn't hear.
I wondered if 'business' would phone again because I'd
always thought George was the standard bearer. Fortunately, life went on, agencies phoned …".

This was a period where the company was in balance.
George's wife Faye inherited George's 51 per cent, but the
week before George died she told John she had terminal
cancer. She died in August. Chris and John looked after her,
because she refused to go into hospital and would not be
treated. There was a long and complicated procedure about
John acquiring the shares, which he did, but that was a
period where he didn't know if TVC would survive.
Everybody was waiting to find out if the company would
live on and if it did whom John would pick to be the creative
head of the studio. Jimmy Murakami and Jack Stokes and
other directors were all hoping, waiting for the nod, but it
never came. John had other ideas. At the time, TVC wasn't
very flush and the complications of getting the shares and
making the company into something secure, gave him the
confidence that he didn't have to replace George; he could
just hire a director for the job in the same way that producers
of live action did. He needed an art director but not a whole
crew of people.

John's era was to be distinctly different than George's simply
because John wasn't an artist himself; but more than that,

the advertising scene was changing and that brought its own very distinct pressures. New players were coming through and TVC, with twenty years experience, was starting to look old hat. They still did the same big campaigns, such as Tony Tiger for Kellogg's Frosties, but the new exciting things were going elsewhere. John had never liked commercials and felt TVC needed a new direction, which is when he decided to make entertainment films that TVC owned. There was money in rights, as Disney had proved ... and as John would eventually prove with *The Snowman*, and the many films afterwards.

John's eventual success as an animation producer was fuelled by a number of contributory factors. 1979 was a year of flux: aside from George's death and John taking the helm at TVC, it was also a year of political change in the UK. Not long after John took over the company, Jim Callaghan's Labour government lost a confidence motion by just 1 vote, forcing a general election. Margaret Thatcher became the first woman Prime Minister, marking the start of the 'Wilderness Years' for Labour (who didn't regain power until 1977). This was important for John because the Tories were to alter the shape of UK broadcasting through the creation of Channel 4, a cultural shift that was about to change his life.

The new channel became the source of a lot of new funding for British animation in general and for John in particular.

Clare Kitson, who commissioned *The Bear* for Channel 4, says John's good nature helps his cause, "that because of his amazing charm and being so likeable, he can get money out of people". And certainly the number of projects he has funded testifies to that. John's pragmatism also helps him bring in the funds for his projects. While some producers might harbour a desire to be one of the creatives on a film, John pushes aside such thoughts. He has input into the story and development of projects, but generally prefers to let the people he is paying do the jobs they're paid to do. This makes for a largely happy workforce and John's people are very loyal.

His skill as a producer is to pick the right people for the job and let them get on with it, at least that is how John pretty much sums up his role. And in an industry somewhat dominated by men, he is known for giving women a chance.

Dianne Jackson , Hilary Ardus, Jo Jo Fryer to name but a few, all got their first break at TVC. So did Clare Jennings, who started off her working life as John's PA many moons ago and recently produced the Oscar winning Aardman film, *Wallace and Gromit and The Weir-rabbit*.

John only chooses projects he is passionate about and has a clear idea of what he wants, and then, more or less, he leaves his team to get on with it. This approach empowers his staff and, as a consequence, they want to do the best for him because they see that he believes in them. His underlying self assuredness that he can and will get the job done means commissioners feel their money is safe in his hands, even if there is somewhat less of it around than when John first produced *The Snowman*.

Throughout all his films, John manages the various obstacles with ease and in his customary way, glossing over the tricky parts and making the whole thing seem effortless. If George Dunning's legacy is a creative one, John Coates' is to take TVC, on the brink of bankruptcy after *Yellow Submarine*, from a service company to globally respected entertainment company. The following pages provide insight into John's modus operandi, what makes him tick, and how he became such a well loved, not to mention successful producer!

11

The Snowman: The First Snow

U ndoubtedly, it was *The Snowman* that confirmed John as a producer of note, establishing him as one of the most respected names in animation. For a half hour film, wordless except for the song 'Walking in the Air', *The Snowman* has done staggeringly well and continues as a global best seller, enthralling new generations of children and families year on year. Still screened every Christmas on the UK's Channel 4, it continues to charm audiences off screen with its stage show, with plans for *The Snowman on Ice* and rumours of a full-length CGI feature.

The film tells the story of James, a young boy who builds a snowman that comes to life, marking the start of a fantastical adventure. James shows his new friend his house and takes him on a motorbike ride, and in exchange, the snowman takes him to a Snowman Ball and to meet Santa Claus. This unique camaraderie cannot last, though, and inevitably the snowman melts, leaving James with just a scarf as a memento of their very special day.

The Snowman was to be the first of many timeless specials John produced that appeal across generations and continents – it is celebrated the world over and has set a new standard in children's broadcasting. Clare Kitson credits it with popularizing the half hour film: "these specials had previously been considered a 'no no' by broadcasters for being too expensive and hard to schedule, but through *The Snowman* John showed they were commercially viable and suddenly everyone was doing them. That kind of increased

James and snowman meets Father Christmas. [© 2010 TV Cartoons Ltd.]

as far as I was concerned, what animation was and where it could be used."

In *The Snowman*, John's 'laissez faire' approach to production works well. He found his talented team and got them to make something wonderful. It is an alchemy he makes look easy when in fact it is the hardest thing to achieve. Norman Kauffman, who rejoined the company post-*The Snowman* and is now a company director, praises John's talents. "He has the ability to pull people together and find their strengths and work with them. His is a can do attitude. If someone says it can't be done, he's just more determined to find a way."

John's seemingly laidback attitude to life belies the fact that TVC work hard and remain, through it all, incredibly professional. Behind the affable and very genuine good disposition, John is also the consummate businessman, who will, for years if necessary, says Norman, "gently persuade his quarry that their book will make a good film, etc. And he always gets them in the end. He picks talent with something distinctive, people who will be experimental, and this builds the team."

Model sheet of Father Christmas, James and the snowman illustrate their relative size.
[© 2010 TV Cartoons Ltd.]

Certainly for *The Snowman*, that the team gelled and could work together was incredibly important. The story of the film dates back to 1978 when Raymond Briggs' book *The Snowman* was first published and caught the eye of Jim Duffy, an American animator then working at TVC. Thinking it would make a good film, he passed it on to John who immediately saw the book's potential. He needed a commission, but these were hard times for small outfits like TVC. UK broadcasters were stingy about investing in domestic animation, preferring to fill their schedules with cheaper US imports. John had almost given up trying to produce his own shows when Channel 4 was mooted, with a remit to support independent British production. John remembers reading the government White Paper (The Broadcasting Act, 1981) the only one he has ever read, and thinking, "that's me, I am independent production".

John now had a way to make his own programmes, but first he needed to option *The Snowman* book rights. Remembering how he had seen it done in the movies, he called up the publisher, Hamish Hamilton, and was put through to the finance director, Iain Harvey, who later became the film's executive producer. Without much haggling, he got a year's option on *The Snowman* for £500, amazing considering the money-spinner the film was to

83

The Snowman..
[© 2010 TV Cartoons Ltd.]

become, and even more amazing because TVC were so naïve about knowing how to get rights, not even having a budget.

Having secured the rights, John then sat on them while he worked on other things, including a one hour special for the US, Castles, directed by John Stokes.

Still, the idea of making a film TVC owned niggled him. With time on *The Snowman* option running out, he thought he had better do something about making the film.

Presenting the story board

The obvious and target broadcaster was Channel 4. Luckily, Raymond's picture book was already storyboard-like. John dispatched two of his assistant animators, Hilary Ardus, who went on to direct *The Bear*, and Jo Jo Fryer, to buy a dozen copies of the book, and start cutting them out to make the board. When there was a spare minute on the camera, they took it to shoot the animatic.

Raymond's original storyline would have only filled 12 minutes of screen time, so John and his team had to embellish scenes to create enough story and action for a half hour special. In the book, the snowman stays in and around James' house, with a brief trip to Brighton pier and back; but this had to change if the film was going to work. The TVC crew conjured up a few story options down the pub, including one where James and snowman fall down a badgers' hole and shared a badgers' tea party ... However, back in the office and sober, they realised this would never do and thought up the trip to the Snowmen's Ball and to meet Father Christmas. They had to cajole Raymond a bit to win him around; he found the idea corny at first, but they did it in the end, and now he is a fan.

The animatic now ran at 7 or 8 minutes and was like a précis for the half hour film. As there were no words, John decided to use library music before presenting to the newly formed Channel 4, but couldn't find any that fitted. Fortunately, he had a lunch with Gerry Potterton, his friend and director of *Heavy Metal*, who had invited along Howard Blake, composer on Ridley Scott's first film *The Duelist* and just becoming known.

Just before John, Gerry and Howard went to lunch, Gerry suggested Howard take a look at *The Snowman* because John needed a bit of music for it. John didn't have much money for original composition but, luckily, Howard said he had just the thing as soon as he saw the animatic. Howard had written the music for a movie some years earlier, but had failed to get that commission so the score had been in a draw for years, waiting for its moment. Sensing a shortage of finance, Howard offered to do "piano to picture for 200 pounds". John said, "you're on", and the music fitted perfectly and turned the animatic into a little bit of magic. Of the three films he worked on for TVC, Howard enjoyed *The Snowman* most. "We met, John, Dianne and I, and a lot of it was joking all the time. It was fun." He recalls how John called him and said the film was three minutes short so they (the snowmen) should go to a party, and asking him if he could write something 'dancey'. "I said yes, and if you come around tonight I'll have it for you. The lightness and joy of the film seemed to touch everyone who worked on it."

Long before they were on air, John took the film, complete with music, to Channel 4 to the "ever-helpful" Paul Madden, commissioning editor who later became a good

Snowman arrives courtesy of Royal Mail.. [© 2010 TV Cartoons Ltd.]

friend and ally on other TVC productions. Everyone loved the film; the PA girls, Paul Madden, Jeremy Isaacs, the new chief executive – *The Snowman* worked its magic touch from the start. It worked well within Channel 4's portfolio because it would contrast with their more edgy programmes. Jeremy Isaacs offered £70,000 there and then, an unheard of amount of money at the time, yet not nearly enough. John summoned up the courage from somewhere, and asked for more. He got it, and was given £100,000, and all this without showing a budget. Iain Harvey got £75,000 out of the publishers, Hamish Hamilton, then an independent company, and later bought by Penguin. That made £175,000 in the kitty and later John re-mortgaged his house for £50,000 to finish the film. There was never a proper budget, yet the broadcasters and publishers parted with money, which astonished all the team, including Howard Blake who cannot imagine such an easy agreement these days.

Having got the 'ok' from Channel 4, John needed a director. In consultation with good friend Jimmy Murakami, he chose Dianne Jackson, who had worked on TVC commercials but never anything long form. Delighted, she jumped at the chance to work on something so special. She talked with John about the idea and saw the animatic, which John explained needed developing into a thirty-minute storyboard: TVC were filming the storyboard as she was drawing it. Unfortunately, Dianne's first bash at the job was way off what John envisaged; she didn't follow the animatic and produced something far too spiritual and serious for his tastes. John, worried things were going badly off-kilter, called Jimmy, who flew in from Dublin to trouble shoot. He saw the early work on the film and had to agree with John, that Dianne was straying off-course. They had a quiet word in her ear and, after that, she was as good as gold and never veered from the animatic again. John says he is immensely grateful to Jimmy for his part in the film, and, of course, *The Snowman* would never have been the runaway success it was without the dedicated talent of Dianne.

John was determined that the film would capture Raymond's signature crayon style used in the book, and pushed Jill Brooks, art director, to find a way to recreate it. TVC were inspired by Frederic Back's technique from *Crac!* and *The Man Who Planted Trees* but achieving the 'crayon' effect proved difficult. Usually an outline was filled with colour, but this was different and had a furry feel to it. The animation had to be controlled or it would have just been a blur and would have "boiled" so much no one would be able to watch it. TVC had to learn how to animate through it, which was painstaking, though eventually Jill Brooks sorted out the whole system. The renderers soldiered away and rendering became a union job afterwards.

John had never discussed with Raymond the nitty-gritty of making the film and Raymond was not really involved beyond the initial agreement. He rather left John and TVC to it, which John appreciated, and Raymond understands why: "I don't think people thought the original author breathing down their necks really helped, and I quite understand that. They didn't shoo me away or anything but I didn't work on it in the slightest degree. I went up to see what they were doing from time to time." Not knowing anything about animation, he was surprised by the intricacies of the production process and was amazed how much work was involved. "I remember going up to the top office in the old TVC building in Charlotte Street, and seeing the room, quite a large room, covered from floor to ceiling with the storyboard." With all this messing about with his storyline, Raymond could have been precious about his work but he was remarkably stoic: "The first thing he saw was the animatic and was really nice about it", says John.

He didn't mutter about Father Christmas then, but I only heard afterwards that before he saw it, he had thought the idea a bit naff. But when he saw it said, "oh gosh, I should have done that in the book".

Channel 4 wanted the film for their opening Christmas as they were going on air in November. By then, it was already February and TVC had to deliver it a month before transmission. To meet the deadline more people came on board, and in the end there was team of up to 70 people working on the film. Production was hectic and the animation team worked day and night to finish. They broke the film up into eight sequences and eight different key animators did the work: Dianne did the entire dance sequence single handed, and planned the whole choreography. The flying sequence, a key part of the film that features the song, was created by a Canadian couple, Steven Weston and Robin White, who had come to John earlier in the year with a documentary about flying over the Canadian countryside. Those flight sequences had impressed John and when he got the film off the ground, and with a nod from Dianne, they flew Steve and Robin from Vancouver. They became part of the team and handled from take off through to landing in the North Pole. It was only later that John thought his film needed something, a song, to bridge the two halves, where James flies off with the snowman.

The song idea came when John went to see the Andrew Lloyd Webber's musical *Cats*. He was not taken with the show, but there was a moment where the music stopped and King Cat, played by Brian Blessed, spoke. John was impressed and it got him thinking. "All the way back in the car that night I kept wondering about a film that was 26 minutes long and not a word, and was that right?" Next day, he phoned Howard and took him to lunch in Charlotte Street, where he explained his thoughts about *Cats*. Howard took John's comments on board and then, "like something out of a Hollywood movie" started to write on a back of a napkin. "And that's how we got *Walking in the Air*", says John. John's touch made all the difference to the final production. He has, as Roger Mainwood puts it: "this uncanny perception to be able to pinpoint that little something that is missing in a film".

At the snowmen's ball.
[© 2010 TV Cartoons Ltd.]

Producing *The Snowman* took a lot of work, but when the cutting copy was ready, John arranged a screening with Jeremy Isaacs and the business half of Channel 4. Understandably nervous as so much hung on the crucial first impression, Dianne and John went along and ran the film. They need not have worried it would be well received; the secretaries had their pocket-handkerchiefs out, people were moved. However, Jeremy Isaacs pointed out to Dianne: "you've made one terrible mistake, my dear: you've only put three buttons on the television set". *The Snowman*, with the extra button on the TV set, went out on Channel 4's opening Christmas 1982 with an audience of half a million viewers.

John was taken aback by what happened next: "We thought we'd made rather a nice film but had no idea it was going to become so huge." Ludovic Kennedy had reviewed *The Snowman* on his 'Did You See' slot on BBC1, which bought the frosty newcomer to a wider public's attention. It was some satisfaction for John Coates to get some kind of payback for the graft he had put in over the years, especially after the financial letdown of *Yellow Submarine*. Since that

89

first broadcast, apart from a hold back for the video release in 1984, Channel 4 have screened *The Snowman* every Christmas since 1982.

And that song: *Walking in the Air*, written by Howard Blake, reached number 5 in the UK pop charts some years later in 1985. Peter Auty sang the original version on the film, but his voice had broken by the time the song charted so Aled Jones sung it on Top of the Pops.

Annecy Animation Festival, June 1983

The year after its debut, TVC were too late to enter *The Snowman* into competition; Annecy was still bi-annual then and Dianne felt it would have spoilt everything to wait another 2 years, so it was shown out of competition. Not that *The Snowman* was short of prizes; its list of awards includes an Oscar nomination in 1984 and the BAFTA Children's Drama award in 1982, robbing the BBC of its previously unblemished record for that prize. This annoyed some BBC executives, but the corporation still wanted him to work with them – he later turned down an offer to produce *The Animals of Farthing Wood* for the BBC and EBU.

Prior to that, during Annecy, 1983, the BBC wanted John to meet the head of publisher Hachette Jeunesse and her husband to discuss funding for TVC's next film. The meeting was held over lunch at the Au Père Bise restaurant, Annecy, on a gorgeous summer day. Tables were laid out on the lawn by the lake and all had an excellent meal and got along great. During the lunch, the conversation turned to converting a mansion in Normandy and John was invited to Normandy for the weekend … Then they got onto the subject of Calvados, always a lively topic for John, and reached that stage of the meal where the Maitre'd was summoned. Next minute, John had three flutes in front of him and three Calvados, 1927, 1929 and 1931: "I had to choose … They all tasted the same to me … So I thought I'd do the obvious and choose the most recent." He was about to take a sip when suddenly, in the middle of all these beautiful surroundings, a girl in a black bikini jumped out of the lake and came up to his table: "We've broken down and Jimmy's run out of fags!" It was Hilary Ardus out in a motorboat with Jimmy Murakami and Howard Blake. The Maitre'd was summoned again, no fuss, and came running back with a sliver salver and a packet of cigarettes, opened. In the meantime, Hilary was chatting to everybody as if this was the most normal thing, says John: "It was just like something out of a James Bond film. Hilary had a good figure; she looked great in a black bikini dripping wet …".

Snowman magic

Over the years, fans and academics and scholars have tried to pinpoint why *The Snowman* is so successful. Howard Blake sees it is a film of transcendence: the notion that we can escape the limitations of life with a sprinkling of magic, the magic of imagination.

For John Coates, the magic comes from the combination of a small boy building something that then comes to life. It captures that dream maybe we all have had– either for a toy, or a dead pet come to life, or a snowman. It is a gentle fantasy, he says: "People build snowmen so Raymond's idea is lovely, but they do melt. And we added a little trick into it, which is the scarf – so although the snowman is no more, the scarf keeps the boy's memories alive. Which is like life, really: we lose people we love but the memories keep them alive."

Fame changed things for the people associated with the film as well as for John. Following its success, Iain Harvey went on to become an animation producer and set up his own studio. Hilary Ardus was later to direct *The Bear*, and Howard Blake achieved considerable success of the back off *The Snowman*. Raymond Briggs found unprecedented interest in his books after the release of the animated film.

Giulietta, an artist in her own right, believes her dad achieving success late in life made her realize that there was no need to be in a hurry, she could allow things to unfold at their own pace. "It (*The Snowman*) feels part of my heritage and the work I did on snow and winter at Central Saint Martins was to a large extent as if I was given permission to, because of *The Snowman*. It was a very taboo project at college because everyone was political and feminist and I wanted to explore winter and depth. So it helped me find my own way of working too, so there are enormous ways I've used his success. The biggest thing for me is that I've never been in a hurry. That is just my dad got successful when he was 50. So that was a big thing for me. So yeah, done lots of showing off!"

The openings …

There have been several different openings since *The Snowman* first aired. Raymond Briggs (live) introduces the original film from the fields behind his house in the Sussex Downs. Dennis Abey (who did the live action on *Yellow Submarine*) was very helpful. "He got a cameraman, a smoke man and his PA and we all drove round to Raymond's house in the very early hours of a morning, just before the trees had started to come out, because we wanted to open on the bare trees and mix dissolve to snow and animation", says John. "It is one of my favourite bits. Dennis filmed Raymond walking up the hill saying, "I remember the day when the snow fell …".

This intro was fine for the domestic UK market but didn't work for the Americans, who wanted a celebrity and were not impressed by the lanky man in his rubber boots – Raymond Briggs. They wanted Julie Andrews, the velvet voiced diva from musicals such as The Sound of Music and Mary Poppins. Julie turned them down in a charming letter, explaining that the film was so lovely she could do nothing to improve it. America still insisted on a celebrity. At that time, TVC were talking to David Bowie about music for *When the Wind Blows*, because he had wanted to do it, though in the end had too many commitments by the time the production deal was agreed. John asked him if he would do the opening for *The Snowman* and he agreed; though finding time in his schedule was not that easy. In the end, he faxed over word that he was going to be in London for the next few days and could spare half a day for filming for $25,000, and John agreed to that.

To do the shoot, under Jimmy Murakami's direction, TVC had to build a set, get a script, and work out what they were going to do with their star. David Bowie, aka Ziggy Stardust but not on that day, arrived at the studio and walked through the front door with just his chauffer. His agent had previously said he would have a sandwich in his dressing room, but when he had finished the shoot, in a small studio in Charlotte Mews, he came and joined the rest of the gang for lunch. As well as his paycheck, he took away the original scarf, hand knitted by the indomitable Ellen Hall who ran TVC's accounts. The Bowie opening sequence became the American version.

The most recent opening, for the films 20th anniversary, featured none other than Raymond Briggs' very own Father Christmas. Raymond wasn't very worried about being filmed himself for the opening years ago, but he was a bit concerned about using Father Christmas. "He was a bit, oh, eh. But then he came round", says John.

The latest version also gave John the chance to alter the end of the film. John always wanted a few flakes of snow after the melting to indicate hope; a new beginning … but originally there was not enough time or money. With the launch of the 20th anniversary DVD, he finally got his wish. It is very important to him, explains Roger Mainwood: "He told me of when he was shopping in Hamleys', the famous London toy store. A video of *The Snowman* was playing and a very young boy was watching the end of the film, entranced. As the boy in the film knelt down in front of his melted snowman friend the child who was watching burst out crying, and John told me how he turned away thinking "oh dear what are we doing with these little films that we are making".

Snowman brand

Today, "*The Snowman*" is a brand, a global money-spinner as famous in Japan as the UK. In the rush to make money from the property, it seems that no merchandising opportunity has been overlooked and in fact perhaps the property is now over-exploited – there are 'Snowman' chicken nuggets, toilet rolls … Someone even once asked for the license to make a Snowman condom. TVC said no. Apart from that, there seems no limit to the licensing of the brand. The commercial side of things is handled by Snowman Enterprises, who've done a lot to take *The Snowman* from screen to stage: the snowman treads the boards, dances a mean pirouette in the *The Snowman* ballet and, if rumours are true, will soon be a CGI feature film. Add to this a plethora of merchandising and more versions of 'Snowman' plush toys, memorabilia, etc, than you could dream of and it is sure "*The Snowman*" brand still has a long way to go.

12

Post Snowman

W ith the success of *The Snowman*, Channel 4 clamoured for a sequel, and John and Raymond were adamant that was not going to happen, as Raymond said, "he melted!". John's view hasn't changed since then: "You can't repeat *The Snowman* and do it better and if you try, you will fall flat on your face." Though he did give an answer to Channel 4's demands for a sequel to *The Snowman*, namely *The Bear* (page 149).

The success of *The Snowman* had taken everyone by surprise, John especially. The big change for him as a consequence was after years of producing for other people suddenly he owned the rights, or at least a good share of them. "It's made me richer and able to relax because there's always a steady income", he admits. On a more general level, he had proved that the half hour special could be commercially successful, and that producers didn't always need to make series. They could indeed make a one off piece.

There were other Snowman spin-offs for John. Suddenly, after the rave reviews and general acknowledgement within the industry, everyone wanted him to produce their shows, but John had waited so long to make his own films, he wasn't about to change tack now; the BBC/EBU *Animals of Farthing Wood* was just one of many job offers he turned down.

The Snowman's international success meant John was in demand at many events worldwide. The US embraced the film wholeheartedly, and John recalls being flown to Boston, British Airways business class, by PBS who had shown *The Snowman* and took the rights for three years. PBS Boston, the most successful of all the PBS channels, had a huge seminar on their own turf as an initiative to galvanise

John posing at the Lac de Sainte Croix, near where he now lives in Provence.
[© 2010 John Coates.]

broadcasters and sponsors to improve the quality of children's films. The congressman, chairman of Ford Motor Company, was the major speaker and there were thousands of people there. They showed one film as the example of the perfect children's film and John felt immensely proud it was *The Snowman*. "Thank God I didn't have to say anything, even though the film got enormous applause."

With all this high-octane success, John was determined to still have his life away from the studio. Especially, he wanted to enjoy time with Chris and this meant travelling together as much as possible, sometimes to exotic locations but often to their beloved Provence, where John now has a house. These sojurns fuelled John and Chris's relationship, whether a few days or one of their more exotic vacations, just being out of the routine kept the spark between the couple. John liked to combine working away with holidays whenever he could and Advertising Film Festival in Cannes, which still takes place in the last week in June, became a

95

The Au Père Bise, Annecy, where Hilary came out of the lake like a James Bond siren in her black bikini.
[© 2010 John Coates.]

regular fixture in their diary, even though John found the event a bit overbearing in some ways and was not a big fan of the advertising world.

While John was enjoying a happy successful life, Bettina, who he had never divorced, was going from bad to worse. She had never got over the shock of his leaving and was given to erratic mood swings. "She was very unhappy one minute, very high the next, and really impossible to live with", explains Giulietta, "but everyone adored her".

In truth, Bettina had already started to become a bit of a high wire before John left and this certainly contributed to his leaving. Later, it would come out she had suffered an incredibly difficult childhood and had always been fragile as a result. Giulietta only realised the extent of it shortly before she died. "I somehow always knew; it was the age of broken homes and everything. I had the sense of that, having had a perfectly happy childhood." Despite her mum's deterioration, Giulietta never judged her father for leaving her and the family home. "I never really saw my father as a bad man, the way a lot of people might see their father under the circumstances." Indeed, by now at Art College, Giulietta had more admiration for her father than anything. She was living around a lot of dysfunction and also realised that her mum was a lot more grounded than a lot of people she went around with. At the same time, she wanted things to get better with Chris. "I tried to make her see that, that I was never really very angry. What was far more disappointing was that somehow we hadn't seen more of each other, so that she could get rid of her animosity. I just wanted her to be nice and relax and be herself."

Nicola, who had now married Adam and had started up a video production business with her husband, felt the same. They both wanted to make things better and if they could not be one big happy family, at least go some way to attempting it. Sadly, they never really became close with Chris, though the two girls gradually grew closer to their father. Like her younger sister, Nicola was also proud of his achievements and while not having plans to follow him into animation, did have a keen interest in media through her own business. Initially, her company was doing well but sadly, Adam developed MS and ended up in a wheelchair. "Obviously, she had to put aside her own dreams and ambitions and be pragmatic, and focus on looking after Adam and her children Ben and Clio who've grown up as a couple of bright individuals."

With the success of *The Snowman*, John was able to relax more; he spent his leisure time riding his horse through the Kent countryside, or holidaying with Chris in his beloved Provence, where he now spends a good portion of the year.

At work, there were many notorious lunches, often dealmakers or deal breakers, or sometimes just to catch up. John's lunches segue into his work relationships; animation is a people business, and networking is an integral part of finding work and keeping it. Not that John struggled there; *The Snowman* was and still is a hot property, and everyone in the industry wanted a piece of the man who made it so, it seemed.

John had to pick his next project carefully; there would have been unfavourable comparisons if he chose anything too similar and the industry was watching to see what he did next.

Luckily, he found what he was looking for ...

13

When the Wind Blows

T he same year *The Snowman* was released, 1982, England went to war with Argentina over the Falkland Islands. John didn't make a film as a comment on that war, but he did later get the opportunity to comment on nuclear war with a film based on Raymond Briggs' book, *When the Wind Blows*. He had been anti-nuclear war since his army days and the devastating attacks on Hiroshima and Nagasaki, so the film was a chance to show something of the horror of nuclear war, vividly depicting its consequences for ordinary folk.

John and Raymond had forged a strong bond during production of *The Snowman*, so it was not surprising the two collaborated again when there was opportunity. *When the Wind Blows* is an altogether darker film depicting what happens to people following government guidelines in the event of nuclear war. Written in the cold war era, when there was talk aplenty of the US and the red button, it is the darkest and most sombre of Raymond's books. At first glance, the film might seem an unusual choice for a company who had just started to make its reputation in 'family films'. Yet TVC had previously gone to the edge with the psychedelic odyssey *Yellow Submarine*, and had refused to opt for a safe ending with *The Snowman* – he was always going to melt!

This fearlessness with his subject is typical of John, says Roger Mainwood, as his ability to see what lies beneath a particular story. "John saw that at the core of the book *When the Wind Blows* was a love story. It is a very dark work, but a wonderful sense of humour and joy of life also runs through the film." Perhaps, Roger ventures, this mirrors John's own way of looking at the world. "Maybe without consciously knowing it, he has weaved his attitude to life into the films he has made and secured them as a fond memories for so many people, a legacy which will surely last for a very long time."

Released in March 1986, *When the Wind Blows* instantly gained attention as a hard-hitting anti-war film. As an introduction, the newsreel footage of CND campaigners and anti-nuclear protests vividly depicts the political social context at the time, backed by David Bowie's powerful title song; while Roger Waters' bleak and uncompromising score emphasizes the horrifying descent into hell of Jim and Hilda Bloggs, two stoic Brits that are based on Raymond's own parents. Naïve, they try to prepare for nuclear war using the ridiculous guidelines contained in the British government pamphlet Protect and Survive: "stock up on food, take off the door and lean it at 60 degrees and hide under it …".

Raymond had given John a mock up copy of the book just before Christmas, 1982, but he didn't read it until Boxing Day, when he was recovering from the flu. Chris came into the bedroom to find him propped up in bed, tearful, and thought it was because he felt unwell. He explained he was fine, just moved by the book, and when he got over his flu a couple of days later, got straight on the phone to director Jimmy Murakami, convinced it was his kind of film and he ought to direct it. He told him he was sending him an amazing book and whizzed it off to him.

Jimmy loved the book and was delighted John wanted him to direct it; not only was he a great fan of Raymond Briggs' work, he also had personal reasons for wanting to direct the film: Hiroshima, the world's first nuclear bomb. "It bought everything very close to home, being Japanese and everything", he explains. "I was in camp and they only rang the bell twice: once when President Roosevelt died and the second time when they dropped the bomb. It was very close to me. I lost a relative at Hiroshima so had always wanted to make a film about nuclear war, not necessarily animated, because I thought the subject matter was too delicate. But Raymond, how he wrote it, the comedy, was absolutely perfect to get the message across to a mass audience".

Sir John Mills and Dame Peggy Ashcroft who did such a wonderful job with the voices of Jim and Hilda Bloggs.
[© 2010 John Coates.]

The Snowman's success no doubt helped John immensely with funding for *When the Wind Blows*. He brought on Hamish Hamilton's former finance director, Iain Harvey, and with his help, got back in touch with Channel 4. Paul Madden, commissioning editor, loved the film idea, and so did Jeremy Isaacs and Justin Dukes, who was the business boss, who immediately put up a budget of £1.7m pounds, quite modest for the quality of the work needed but enough for TVC to get going with the film.

They had the director, the money and, as with *The Snowman*, wanted to recreate the look of the book for the film. With just two characters, the voice cast would be critical; it needed to be a working class accent, not the cut glass tones of so many actors/actresses of a certain age.

For the voice of Hilda Bloggs there was no doubt whom TVC would like and that was Dame Peggy Ashcroft. With her left wing inclinations, they had no trouble in getting her, but finding a voice for Jim proved more difficult.

John and Jimmy had various meetings, lunches, and talked to many people to ensure they found the right cast. Initially, he approached Richard Attenborough, then Chairman of C4, for Jim, and was told he was too busy to help, although John doesn't know how much he was actually involved in that decision. A second choice was Sir John Mills, who lived in Denham village. John rang and spoke to his wife, who nicely explained he was mowing the lawn at one end of the garden, but would come back up if he could hold on … The two John's finally had their phone call and soon afterwards had lunch with Iain Harvey, at Antoine's, a fish restaurant in Charlotte Street and very close to TVC and Channel 4. Sir John was enthused by the project but had to leave for a meeting with Dickie (Attenborough), who had been first choice to voice Jim. John Coates thought it would be embarrassing if Sir John mentioned the lunch and found out that Sir Richard had been offered the part first, so he said, "it's funny that because we were thinking of Dickie Attenborough", and Sir John said, "Ahh, So I'm second choice am I?". The film went on to achieve critical acclaim and John (Coates) believes part of its success was an excellent voice cast.

The actual voice recording for the two of them (John Mills and Dame Peggy) was booked for three days. As often happens, there were some initial tribulations and worries, but the two stars got on and John recalls "settled into their voices in no time at all". By the third day they were almost done, and stunned John and the sound crew when they did the whole last take straight off, without a practice take. "The sound recording people and ourselves, a little group in there, broke into applause as if we were in the theatre." John can't imagine two people who would do it better: "It was a fantastic anchor on the animation side. We could fasten anything to it."

After their stellar performance, the two stars decided not to go out to lunch so sandwiches were bought in and they all

Hilda and Jim Bloggs without backgrounds. TVC kept very true to Raymond Briggs' original designs. [© 2010 TV Cartoons Ltd.]

had a little glass or two of wine. It turned out this grand old English actor and actress had never appeared in film or the theatre together, but they had appeared in David Lean films and spent the time reminiscing about his extravagances, which kept everyone entertained.

Meantime, Jimmy, in Cannes on other business, was busy roughing out the storyboard and sending TVC parcels of rough drawings, which were handed to Richard Fawdry the art director and Joan Ashworth, who drew them and pinned them up. They filled the room and set the standard, creating an impressive storyboard, which Jimmy went through when he got back from Cannes. Raymond Briggs came in and helped complete the dialogue, pinned up underneath the pictures. The finished board was presented to Jeremy Isaacs, Paul Madden and the C4 people, and the production got underway.

Jimmy and John (Coates) wanted to be faithful to the book

but also to bring some dimension into it, as they had done with *The Snowman*. So the image would not look flat, they built a model house and shot stop frame on it for all the backgrounds. Like that, they could turn them and travel from one room to another, which to do by hand in animation would have been time consuming and hugely expensive.

They filmed with Ken and Mary (Ken Friswell ARS Background System Producer and Mary Evans his Camera Operator) and were booked in their studio for 11 weeks. Jimmy, very painstakingly, directed all the separate little scenes. It was very tricky matching the model with the animation. "You have a model tea cup on the table in the stop-frame set up, which then has to be matched with Jim or Hilda picking it up to blend it into the film", says John.

For the backgrounds, shot on stop frame, the production team needed to be able to print them up as stills on which to lay the animation. Problem was all the pictures had to match exactly on the peg bars so they didn't jiggle about, which proved so tricky that TVC invented a gadget to solve the difficulty. No doubt over a lunch, John pressed and said we've got to sort this out, and as he puts it: "let the brains think how this was going to be done". In the end, they set up a photographic enlarger, and put a Mitchell camera registration gate inside it – reckoned to be the steadiest and best in existence. It worked magically; each day the model shoot would be processed through and the backgrounds would come in all ready in registration. John was very pleased with the outcome: "There are lovely scenes of Jim and Hilda going from room to room and turning the rooms and things, and that really helped the film enormously". As often happens, the production was fairly fraught: at the very end, there was a small team of people working day and night to finish the final artwork, but it turned out well, in no small part, says John, thanks to the young protege Ian McCue. "He rose to the occasion and helped rally the crew. Ian went on to become one of the best production coordinators on future TVC films.

Regrettably, the extra detail did notch up the budget and John had to call in the completion guarantors to finish the film. "Luckily, they proved very sympathetic, and didn't try to control us and let us finish it in our own time", says John.

Jimmy Murakami, director of When the Wind Blows. *[© 2010 John Coates.]*

"In the end, the film went over two hundred thousand pounds, which in those days was a little bit more than it is now, but still not a terrifying amount."

John's producer's kudos was enhanced by *When the Wind Blows*, which was critically acclaimed and won a number of awards. The premier was a very exciting affair in London. "The distributors housed us with our wives at The Ritz Hotel, I remember we had afternoon tea there with Raymond and Iain Harvey and myself and we all had an extraordinary evening. The premier was at the big ABC cinema in Shaftsbury Avenue, and was attended by celebrities."

The film went off and into release and did moderately well for such a dark subject. Raymond is a fan of the film.

Acknowledging it was a difficult thing to do, he says it is "extremely good", on the whole, though he thought Dame Peggy Ashcroft a mite too posh for Hilda, and is not a fan of the erotic thoughts scene, directed by Dianne Jackson . "I didn't particularly like Hilda seeing herself as a fairy, she flits about with fairy wings. Everyone is meant to laugh at her big fat bottom. She wouldn't think of herself like that; that was a mistake in the thinking. It was just laughing at her really, which I didn't like."

Years later, a taxi driver picking John up from the studio noticed the plaque of *The Snowman* and asked if he had anything to do with animated films. He said there was a film he saw some years ago, which was the best animated-film ever, about two old people faced with a nuclear war. John remembers saying: "That was *When the Wind Blows*, and that was a film we produced. 'Ahha,' said the taxi driver. "Marvelous".

John considers *When the Wind Blows*, "one of the best films I was involved in, and quite dear to my heart in many ways". Unfortunately, the film never did as well as it might in America because they thought it was a children's film, which of course it was not. John's still cross about that: "They made a proper mess of distribution in America. We might have actually made some money if we'd done better there". John still finds it special: "It was one of the best films Jimmy Murakami directed, and there was a lot of talent involved in the making of it. And certainly a lot of passion."

About the time of the premiere there was a screening at BAFTA for politicians and John remembers giving a dreadful speech. If the film had a result, it was the government quickly withdrew their ridiculous "what to do in the event of a nuclear war" pamphlet. "Quite right", says John. It was a load of nonsense."

When the Wind Blows went on to win the Chicago Film Festival and won Best Feature Film at Annecy, 1987.

14

Life Matters, Becoming a Grandpa and Holidaying in Kenya

The year *When the Wind Blows* won its coveted awards, the wind blew literally, the famous hurricane of 1987, and also metaphorically when there was a massive stock market crash: Black Monday, where the values of stocks plummeted. Despite its growing success, TVC was privately owned and didn't suffer any fall out from this financial disaster, though Black Monday's effects were to ricochet through the UK economy, eventually bringing recession.

For the time being, though, John was in a good position after the success of his first two films. He could have played it safe after *The Snowman* and picked a second film as gentle as his first, but *When the Wind Blows* as a follow through paid dividends for him and TVC. Having avoided typecasting with the latter, he was rapidly earning an industry reputation as a producer who delivered the goods and was not afraid to take risks. After so long wanting to make his own films and being unable to, now on a roll, he was keen to get on with the next one; but he could afford to be picky and rather than do the first thing offered to him, chose to wait a while. At the same time, he was in demand to speak about *The*

John having breakfast in the Masi Mara - Kenya.
[© 2010 John Coates.]

Snowman and attended various festivals and events. With producers and broadcasters vying for him to produce their projects, he had a full diary and was lauded wherever he went.

John enjoyed his work but wasn't obsessed with it. He wanted to keep a balance between TVC and home and enjoyed spending time at his house in Kent, walking his dog and pottering about in the garden. Soon, his family life was to change considerably – he became a grandfather for the first time when Nicola gave birth to Ben in the early part of 1988. John was delighted, even though he had never had a son so baby boys were new to him.

Sometime after Ben was born and in the lull between projects, he took a holiday, as always somewhere off the beaten track – he hates touristy places. Not sure where to go, he decided on Kenya after hearing good reports about the place. A fellow traveler advised him not to book but to fly to Nairobi, take a room in the Norfolk Hotel and tell the people there that he wanted to go North to Treetops and South to the Masai Mara, a large park reserve in South-Western Kenya, and then on to the coast. The only empty room the Norfolk hotel had was the bridal suite, so John booked it, at some enormous cost. It was a lovely hotel, relics of empire, now run by friendly black Africans.

It transpired that he could drive up North, as it was safe tribal territory all the way. John and Chris took a four-wheel drive up there, only to find at the end of it that Treetops (literally a hotel in the treetops) was closed. It had been burnt down, much to their bitter disappointment.

John in Nairobi ready to fly to the Masi Mara in a Canadian built Dakota that had flown coal in to Berlin during the airlift.
[© 2010 John Coates.]

Plan B was a place called the Ark, as in Noah's ark. It was like a ship in a way, near a waterhole where patrons could dine in the jungle. "Diners could sit and have dinner and watch the animals come to quench their thirst or take a bath. If any came in the night, one time a rhino came down, the hotel staff alerted the guests", explains John. "There were little speakers in the room, and everyone came running down to see the rhino", which he loved, "to be that close to one that wasn't in a zoo". After that, he and Chris stayed in the country club, where no expense was spared, and then drove the jeep back to the Norfolk hotel to stay as arranged. Next morning, they flew to the Masai Mara on an old Dakota plane – it had been built in Canada during the war, and then flown coal into Berlin during the famous airlift. "It had its whole history written at the front of every seat, and was one of those old planes that takes off on a wing and a prayer ... Those old planes go up very slowly, just clear the trees at the end of the runaway ... Chris couldn't look she was so afraid." They landed on this tiny little strip and were picked up by a Toyota four-wheel drive and taken to an area known as the Governors' Camp. Next there was a river crossing, more than a bit scary with crocodiles on the bank. They saw lions in close up, but luckily well fed so they were sleepy! The couple spent a week there, in great comfort

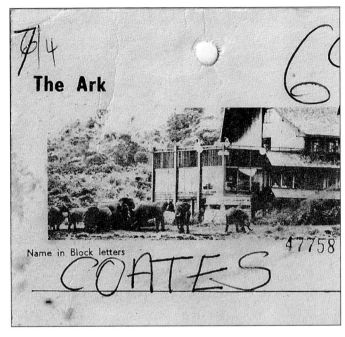

considering they were in the jungle. The tents were lovely, with a shower and very comfy. The food was delicious and there was an excellent tented restaurant, with on going barbecue and fried eggs in the morning.

For dinner in the evening, John had to wave a big torch, "so the hotel staff would take you to the restaurant and then escort you back after dinner. One evening, there was a giraffe standing behind John and Chris's tent. "It was amazing. You did sort of think I am in Africa." One of the nights, a whole herd of hippopotamus stampeded right through the camp, waking everyone up. Next morning, there were huge footprints right through the middle of the camp and everyone realised they had a narrow escape. After the week there, which included a daily excursion looking at wild animals, they flew back for another night at the Norfolk Hotel and then took a proper plane to Mombasa, quite a long flight to the coast, at least an hour and a half or so … When they arrived in Mombasa they hired a car and went north. John recalls a very pretty girl, born in Kenya but English family, recommended trying out the Ocean club on the coast. They did and had a great time. It was informal and the food was nice, even if bad weather spoilt their fun a little.

109

"There had been a huge storm before we arrived and the swimming pool had been filled up with sand, which was a shame. We used the swimming pool of the hotel down the road, and the ocean was lovely ...".

Chris by jeep in Kenya. [© 2010 John Coates.]

Nicely tanned and somewhat rested, John returned back to England and to TVC only to find Bettina had gone steadily downhill. Despite the family's attempts to help her, she was too far gone, and sadly died. It is a reality John still has problems with. He had never expected the split to hit her as hard as it did, and had been convinced that at some point, she'd rally round, snap out of it ... all the clichés. She died on January 3rd, 1989.

His daughters were by now in their early thirties. They were devastated by their mother's death, of course, but they didn't spin round in anger and blame their father for the way things had turned out. There was no acrimony; it was all in the past and they were interested in the here and now. Giulietta, especially, was driven at this time to get on with her art, and then John proved to be an inspiration to her more than anything else. He had found success late in life and that was not lost on her. She could work at her own pace; there was no rush.

15

Granpa

Some time later, John was sitting at his desk in the TVC offices in Charlotte Street when the phone rang. It was Tom Maschler, then the boss at Jonathan Cape, asking him to come view a book he was sure had the makings of an amazing film. He asked John if he could come over straight away, and as it was a nice sunny morning and the publisher was in Bedford Square, just ten minutes away, John said he would. When he got there, Tom Maschler had all the original artwork (by John Burningham) laid out on the carpet so John got on his knees to look at it closely. He liked what he saw but as he got near the end of looking at the pictures said, "I can see something awful is going to happen ..." (meaning that Granpa is going to die). That didn't put him off; the snowman had melted, after all. In fact, the meeting went better than well and a deal was agreed there and then. John Burningham was happy that publisher and producer made a deal so easily – unlikely to happen today, he says, with everything run by committee.

John saw in *Granpa* a chance to make a beautiful moving film and sought ways to explore the melancholy underlying theme of loss without schmaltz or tackiness; fitting given he was dealing with his own personal thoughts on the matter following Bettina's death.

So far, the snowman had melted, Jim and Hilda Bloggs had climbed into a sack and succumbed to the grim reaper, and Granpa was going to die, leaving his granddaughter to feel his absence. Yet of the three films, *Granpa* is the one people can most relate to because it's a person dying, not a snowman melting, and the death isn't a spectacular one caused by a nuclear bomb, rather the end of a life well lived.

Aware that time is short, 'granpa' wants to leave happy memories for his granddaughter Emily by telling her wonderful, fantastical stories. Journeying to imaginary far away lands, they battle fiery dragons and dense jungles. Eventually, the awful day arrives when Emily arrives at granpa's house, only to find he is gone for good.

Signed photograph of Dianne's animation team for Granpa - standing outside the front door of Charlotte Street studio.
[© 2010 TV Cartoons Ltd./Granpa Ltd.]

Excited to be working on another fabulous project, John wanted to do something different and decided to make a musical. He hired Paul Madden as executive producer and together they went to Channel 4 and raised 50 per cent of the budget. Dianne Jackson agreed to direct and Howard Blake was commissioned to score the music. They had worked out so well on *The Snowman* and seemed a natural choice. Howard found the project dark at first, but John talked him around. About a month or so later, John remembers taking Dianne and Howard to lunch at Othellos, to a little table in the window. There, in a complete U-turn, they told him they didn't think it would make a good film

112

at all: it was too dark and they were not going to proceed with it. John spent the next hours convincing them otherwise: "I think we left that table at about six o clock that evening, by which time I'd talked them back into it and we never looked back".

No doubt John's tenacity to get the film he wanted helped immeasurably; that people tend to want to give their best to his productions helped some more. Author/ illustrator John Burningham, who met John when he first came to view his book, *Granpa*, noticed that John inspires loyalty in his staff and could get the best out of them: "he obviously is somebody who commands a sort of allegiance with the team of people who work on these things. He jollies them along but knows exactly what's happening: he probably is cracking the whip but you wouldn't know it."

One way he cracked the whip on *Granpa* was by dictating, "No fuss potting", during the production. It was his way of saying get on with things and was directed at Loraine Marshall and Richard Nye at the start, "he just got used to using it and labelled various people Fusspot number 1, Fusspot number 2, etc.", says Loraine. "I don't remember anyone taking the titles seriously; everyone just continued to do their jobs as well as possible. I expect anyone who was checking got called it, even though that was the nature of their work."

Adapting John Burningham's book into a film was always going to be complex, even for a seasoned producer like John. He and Dianne agreed the best way to deal with it was to break it down into sections, each with a different animator, same as they had done on *The Snowman*. There were ten sections in all, with ten animators, including Neville Astley, Mark Baker, Dave Unwin, Jack Stokes, Arthur Butten, and Steve Weston, with Dianne Jackson overseeing the whole thing. Like *The Snowman*, where John added the song, he added his own touch to *Granpa*, as he has in many of his films; it's such touches that can make all the difference to a production. *Granpa*, he felt, needed uplifting at the finish to stop it being maudlin, so he suggested that Emily was reunited with her recently-deceased Granpa in her imagination, bringing hope to an otherwise sad end.

Something of a coup, John got Peter Ustinov to voice Granpa; he was perfect for the part, and also a wonderful

113

raconteur. John recalls they were having lunch at The Jardin du Gourmet in Greek Street with Sarah Brightman, who sung the end-title song 'Make Believe'. "She was in a Mini with her filo-fax and taking everything seriously. TVC was also taking things seriously; we just don't tend to show it, but we do", says John. "Peter Ustinov was his usual self, telling his stories and joking, but Sarah Brightman wasn't going to waste time and snapped her filo-fax together. She sped off and Peter Ustinov lent forward and said, 'tell me, who was that young lady?'".

The film came out but Peter never saw it because he was away in Hollywood. Back in England and being knighted, TVC got in touch with his agent and asked if he would like to see the film. He said he would so they arranged a screening in Dean Street. It was the day after he had been knighted and John recalls, "We all laid on the heavy sir". Sir Peter said: "What you people don't know is when you're knighted you get sent a bit of paper to tick where appropriate. I can kneel or I can't kneel, but they don't leave a space to say, I can kneel but I can't get up again!'"

TVC's Unicef World Premiere of Granpa. [© 2010 TV Cartoons Ltd./Granpa Ltd.]

Granpa made its television debut on Channel 4 on New Year's Eve 1989 at 6.30pm and went on to win the Prix Jeunesse in 1990. It is now part of the Disney catalogue. When ITV licenses came up for renewal, TVS, who had co-financed and held the broadcast rights with Channel 4, lost their license in December 1992 and sold off their film library; "so *Granpa* went through MTM, Family Channel and Fox Kids, which was bought by Disney and sadly, languishes in their vast archives", says John. "In fact it has never been seen in the US in any form or in a large part of the world, which is a shame because it is a really lovely film."

16

The Seychelles ...

As ever, with another film in the can, John took a bit of time out to travel, except this time it was necessity as well as pleasure. Professionally, things were going well for him; they could have hardly been going better – *The Snowman* was still going strong and every film John had made since further added to his reputation as producer of excellence. If he didn't have the Midas touch, he was darn close: the money was coming in, everything was going swimmingly … and then Chris got sick.

She was diagnosed with ME, back then hardly heard of, and started to deteriorate pretty quick, soon becoming too weak to ride her horse. Worried sick, John sent her to The Priory for consultation and hopefully a cure. She had some treatment, which John thought fairly feeble, but she seemed to steady up after it. Afterwards, the doctor prescribed a lovely long holiday, a minimum of three weeks. Luckily, money wasn't an issue, so he followed a friend's advice to try the Seychelles, via a posh travel company that recommended a wonderful hotel with a room right by the seashore. John booked it for a week.

The hotel was on Pralin, the Seychelles' second biggest island and for John in many ways the prettiest; it was wild, with a handful of nice hotels and nearby (about 5 miles) La Digue, the fourth smallest island. John and Chris planned to take the schooner across to the hotel on La Digue, which was so exclusive that guests were limited to a five-day stay.

A bicycle came with their hotel room. The island has no traffic, so a buffalo cart took tourists down to the scooner, about a half-mile from the hotel. Pralin had just dirt tracks, no roads as such. "I hadn't ridden a bike for years that's a

fact, but we could whiz about on our bicycles. It was a very exclusive holiday; just two other couples on this great white beach of sand and polished black rock of the headlands, and palm trees ... The sand was lovely with a steep shelf so you could swim straight away."

Some parts of Pralin were less accessible than others and there was a bay rumoured to be something a bit special. Intrigued, John and Chris hired a Mini Moke so they could see what all the fuss was about, but had to abandon their effort when the Moke, which lacked four-wheel drive, couldn't make the steep climb to the top of the path that led on to the bay. Next morning, they hired a Suzuki Jeep and managed to get to the bay, which was beautiful and had an arrow nailed to a tree pointing the way to go. They followed it to a sign, which John presumed was to go to the beach, which read park here and sound your horn. They did as asked and then waited. Not long afterwards, from a headland about half a mile out, a little boat came chugging up, picked them up and took them out. Fantastic! They ended up at quite a small restaurant hidden behind a waterfall, where the main meal was fish, very fresh fish! An Australian who had married a local girl ran the place and did well enticing the well heeled-travelers who ventured to his little spot.

After lunch, John, a strong swimmer, felt like taking a dip. Seeing the way the boat had come, he could clearly see where the rocks were and feeling adventurous said he'd swim back. Chris said he was mad, but John was sure he was perfectly safe. He was, apart from a Conger eel that lurked under the steps, at least that's what the Australian said, who cautioned it was best to dive from the little boat moored nearby.

"No problem", said John, and did just that, only to come a cropper when he made his perfect swan dive and his knickers got caught on some oars stacked in the boat (they were stacked long ways and sideways). John swam back to shore naked. When he got back, Chris, who had gone back in the boat, was there with her camera and snapped John coming on to the beach just about covering his embarrassment.

The trip did Chris the world of good and she improved quickly afterwards, indulging her hobbies and passions and even picking up a few more along the way. She took up sculpting and made, amongst other things, a bronze of George Dunning's Flying Man. Life was getting simple again for John and he was happy. There was money in the bank, he had a good life with Chris, and he had his family around him.

His career showed no signs of slowing down, far from it. There was always another project to make, another award to add to the groaning weight of those already on the shelf. John was a regular attendee at the TV market in Cannes, known as Mipcom, but that was for all types of programming, not specifically animation. European animation was largely small scale, cottage industry, because its animation houses simply could not compete with America's large scale schematic. That was to change in 1990 with the launch of Cartoon Forum, which fast became a regular fixture in John's diary. He had a full calendar that would soon become fuller still. Run under the auspices of the Media Programme in Brussels, Cartoon Forum, now of many years standing, was a simple idea to facilitate production between smaller independent production companies; by co-producing they could achieve economies of scale and so hopefully allow them to compete with the American market. The idea was the gatherings would take place in outlying areas of Europe, to be as far away from the usual hubbub as possible. John quickly became a big fan of the event, which he has attended numerous times and always enjoys.

117

17

Father Christmas – 1991

E ngland was just heading into recession when John
started on his next film, *Father Christmas*, but TVC
wouldn't suffer from the downturn just yet, even
though a lot of manufacturing based industries were really
suffering. Many in the financial services sector were also
fearful of losing their jobs and probably many in the media
industry, but John had another film to make and could, at
least for the time being, ride the wave.

After the sadness in *The Snowman* and *Granpa*, and the
gloom of *When the Wind Blows*, *Father Christmas* was
altogether a lighter project, especially welcome with all the
dark recession talk at the time. The film was based on
combining two of Raymond's books: *Father Christmas* (1973)
and *Father Christmas Goes on Holiday* (1975), and there was
much joy when John's daughter had a production of her
own – John became a grandfather for the second time when
Nicola gave birth to her daughter Clio in the summer of
1991.

Father Christmas, a hugely irreverent but rib-tickling tale of
Santa on holiday who, after various exploits in Las Vegas,
France and Scotland, finds all the kafuffle so exhausting he
is glad to get back to work delivering Christmas presents …
turned out to be one of John Coates' most commercially
successful films. It is a John Coates film because unlike
other TVC properties, the rights to *Father Christmas* do not
reside in TVC itself, but are owned personally by John, Iain
Harvey and Gower Frost. Gower Frost, who had a

live-action production company, had owned the rights for some years. Much to Raymond's annoyance his publishing company had sold him the rights in perpetuity, which meant that no one else could do anything with them, even if the rights owner had failed to move the film project forward. As a result, the *Father Christmas* books were locked for years.

Eventually, John and Iain were able to sort out an agreement with Gower Frost for the rights, and the latter still owns a percentage of the film. It was Iain Harvey's idea to put the deal together and he did well raising the money, while John was much more involved in putting the crew together and getting the film made. Iain also put in some of his own money. Budgeted at £1.4 million, *Father Christmas* is the most expensive of TVC's half-hour specials. As usual, Channel 4, then with Clare Kitson in the commissioner's chair, put up half of the budget.

Dianne Jackson was to direct but she was too unwell at that point and nominated Dave Unwin to do the job under her supervision. John agreed with her: by then, she had already done the storyboard but was not up to actually going into production. "I think the idea was that Dianne would still be hands on, but I would be in the studio doing the everyday work – you know, the animation", says Dave. In fact she became ill soon afterwards and he took over and became the working director. That was the first time he had that kind

119

of responsibility and that is when he got to know John Coates, and that is when they got to know each other better.

Even without as much of Dianne's input as hoped, *Father Christmas* was a straight-forward film to make. Clare Kitson didn't like the original voice, which was Michael Elphick. She felt he was ill at ease with Father Christmas's idiosyncratic turn of phrase and brought no conviction to the character. So Mel Smith was used instead. After that, things were fine, no problems at all in the UK. The US market was another matter entirely.

Father Christmas book cover.
[© 2010 Picture Puffin]

The Americans didn't want the UK version and as the money in the film was from one of the big cable channels, HBO Showtime, they had some sway. They had seen the book and as usual TVC had done a film storyboard, which they had also seen and approved, adds John, and on that basis TVC went ahead and made the film. Living the producer lifestyle, John was at Hollywood when they viewed it and staying at the Sunset Marquee Hotel, a stone throw from his sister Anne's apartment – she would usually put him up but she had guests so he had to slum it at the Marquee!

John was relaxing by the pool, with glass in hand, when there was a phone call. It was Iain Harvey calling from London with bad news; the Americans had called him over difficulties with *Father Christmas*. "He said there's a list as long as your arm. I think you'd better talk to the lady there direct. It's practically a remake", remembers John, who thought the whole palaver was ridiculous. In his mind, they had seen and approved everything. Iain was sure the Americans would pay for any changes for the US version, as there was uproar internally. John, sitting by the pool, phoned up the lady representing Showtime. He vividly recollects during that particular conversation, where she went down the list of things to change. "She said they could get away with white wine, because it could be mistaken for water, but he (Father Christmas) couldn't be seen drinking red wine … I said, for heaven's sake, he did it in the book."

She said, "no, we don't want any of that ..." "I remember my blood level was rising, and eventually I lost my self control. I said, I know what, it'd be ok if he had a fucking gun ... she said, 'Now John!' "

There are other changes in the US version. In the film and in the book, Father Christmas sits on the loo and has his morning ablutions, so that had to come out, and when he is in Las Vegas, he takes his things off to put on his swimming costume and shows a flash of bare bottom and the Americans would not have that. Worse, the whole Scottish pub scene had to be a coffee bar. The English uncut version sells well in England and worldwide and makes quite a lot of money. The DVD goes pretty well in USA where Columbia Tristar, now Sony, handle it. The film is often seen on Channel 4 at Christmas.

18

Recession

Ry the end of filming *Father Christmas*, the country had plunged into recession. It was the early 1990s and the situation was dire for TVC as it was for other small production companies. There would be no exotic holiday this time, far from it. Fortunately, even in the grip of a downturn, the reliable income from *The Snowman* meant that TVC fared better than most Indies; many had to combine forces to survive the tough times. John saw the importance, especially at this time, in not giving into stress and sought freedom from executive pressure by indulging his love of riding on the grounds near where he lived. The recession limped on for some time and John's somewhat Zen approach to life, having been through hard times before, notably with the *Yellow Submarine*, meant he was able to keep everything together.

Eventually, things took a turn for the better: TVC landed a commission for *Peter Rabbit and Friends*, six x ½ hours, and then the *Wind in Willows* 75 minute feature, more than enough to keep it afloat.

19

Beatrix Potter: 1992–1995

I t's fair to say the Beatrix Potter series arrived in the nick of time for TVC. John hadn't gone out looking to animate the much-loved books, but rather they came to him. In truth the story of the Beatrix Potter series dates back many years previous, when the original publisher Frederick Warne still controlled the author's estate. John was sat at his desk in the TVC offices when he got "the call" from Frederic Warne. Beatrix Potter had aligned with them in the days when women found it very hard to get published, but they were a small company and somewhat on their last legs when they made the call to TVC about developing the characters for animation. So it was that John and *The Snowman* director Dianne Jackson went around to their offices to talk to them about converting the stories into film.

Warne were in touch with two or three studios competing to get the job of animating Beatrix Potter's world and TVC were asked to do some character designs and prep work. They did and a long time went by, at least it seemed to John, before they heard they got the job. And then there was a much longer period of silence, lasting several years, before the project once more came to light. This was when Penguin bought out Warne in 1983, although it wasn't until the 1990s that they contacted John about working on the project.

Having acquired the Beatrix Potter rights, Penguin subsequently set up a division solely to handle the books, publishing and explore film opportunities. The change of ownership didn't badly affect the brand's animation

123

Production drawings for The Tale of Two Bad Mice, produced by John Coates for TVC and directed by Roger Mainwood. [© 2010 TV Cartoons Ltd.]

ambitions, in fact Penguin quickly found £250,000 to develop a feature film. Duly, Hilltop Films (after Beatrix Potter's house in the Lake District) was formed, a co-venture between TVC and Penguin to handle the rights. Dianne Jackson undertook to write a treatment, later developed into a full script by Roger McGough. Hilltop then decided to do some test footage, so they had a bit of finished film to show Warner Bros, who were very interested in the proposed feature film.

It was John's idea, and Dianne's, to incorporate both live action and animation into the film using live action to enter into the story telling. The tests involved Lucy, Beatrix Potter's niece, who was to be used as the live-action thread throughout the film. They tested at Pinewood studios under the direction of Dennis Abey, quite an elaborate test using both live footage and animation, and presented the work to Warner Brothers. Warner Bros liked the test and invited the Hilltop Team to Hollywood. They were flown first class – ready to discuss the whole project. John remembers being swept by limousine to the WB lot and as they were going up the famous staircase with the Casablanca blow-ups, thinking, "we'd really arrived in the movies".

They had a nice meeting with several ladies, the senior one was Jim Henson's daughter, and discussed the script and film treatment. They came up with some good ideas, which John agreed to incorporate into the production. The budget was approved and they left the meeting on a high note, everyone full of good intentions to get rolling with the film as soon as possible.

Then … the first Gulf War started. Warner Brothers got on to Penguin and told them to hold everything until they could see what would happen, but the consensus was the conflict would be over in no time at all. Of course, the Gulf War dragged on and on, and by the time it was over, there

John is seen here with a scene from The Tailor of Gloucester, *directed by TVC's own Jack Stokes. [© 2010 TV Cartoons Ltd.]*

was a new regime at Warner's and they didn't want to pursue the film.

John was never given an official version of why the film idea was shelved, but suspects the real reason probably had something to do with rights – that Warner's wanted more rights than Penguin were prepared to give. For Penguin, Sally Floyer hints that it was more long term considerations than the short term problem of the Gulf War: "we always had some nervousness at our end about the robustness of a Peter Rabbit film, really. We thought it too gentle for a feature. This was long before the 1990s and the explosion of films for children, which began with Disney's *The Lion King.*"

In the end, Penguin decided a film wasn't going to get off the ground and the best way forward was television. Time went by and the Beatrix Potter copyright was running out. Sally Floyer, who ran the division, called up TVC to discuss the situation with John and invited him and Dianne to lunch to discuss possibilities for the Potter brand. They had a long chat about going on to television – which they considered the quickest way of getting definitive characters out and about before the copyright ran out. It was important to act quickly because once copyright expired the floodgates could open for all manner of interpretations on the property.

Penguin initially wanted to make several 15-minute episodes of the best of the Beatrix Potter stories, which didn't sit well with John and Dianne, who preferred half hours as they tended to get the best-broadcast slots. In those pre-London congestion charge days, when London traffic was even more awful than it is now, they got in a taxi, and planned to drop John off at Rathbone Place to go back to the studio in Charlotte Street, and Dianne off at Waterloo station – she lived in the New Forrest. They were 30 or 40 minutes in the taxi and during that time put together a schematic for the films, i.e. they would be half hours. That in some instances, like *Benjamin Bunny* and *Peter Rabbit*, the two stories run together, interlinked anyway, so they could make up the running time. They also thought of the idea of having live action tops and tails to introduce the stories, to introduce Beatrix Potter and to set the feeling of where she lived up in the Lake District to give the thing a certain mood.

A short time later, with all this on paper, they went back to see Penguin and Sally Floyer, who loved the classic, hand-drawn designs that had stayed true to Potter's own vision. She also was a fan of the live-action element, which John had first suggested for the film and was pleased with TVC's format for the whole thing. "It's nice because the audience can see Hilltop, they can see Beatrix Potter herself and they can see how the stories came to be. And we wanted that", she explains. "We wanted people to see Beatrix Potter as the creator of stories and not just the stories themselves, because that really lifts them up, puts them in a special spot."

John and TVC's vision came into being bit by bit. Pearson, who owned Penguin, fully funded the venture and, as per John's suggestion, they selected several studios to each make one or two films, all under the general direction of John as producer and Dianne Jackson as the overall director.

The first six films were: *The Tale of Peter Rabbit and Benjamin Bunny*; *The Tale of Samuel Whiskers or The Roly Poly Pudding*; *The Tale of Tom Kitten and Jemima Puddle-Duck*; *The Tailor of Gloucester*; *The Tale of Pigling Bland*; *The Tale of Mrs.Tiggy-Winkle and Mr. Jeremy Fisher*. Penguin wanted them finished in two years; and had put the pressure on because the copyright was running out. Today, trademark is more important that copyright and in fact not long after

Penguin gave the go-ahead for the TV specials, copyright was extended from 50 to 70 years after an author's death.

There was no way TVC could make six half hours in two years; it was beyond their capacity. They needed help, so John and co went out lunching friends and competitors and eventually roped in Grand Slamm Animation, who then were Ginger Gibbons and Geoff Dunbar, and also seconded the help of Jill Brooks' animation and Mike Stuart (Stuart Brooks). They agreed to do two films each, which was one a year; the half hours take nine months. Under Dianne's control, each studio would write scripts and present film storyboards and animatics for approval. The other studios were commercial companies that didn't have experience in entertainment features, though after the Beatrix Potters' success they did in turn start to produce their own non-advertising animation. It was a great way for the chosen studios, who John thought all performed marvelously, to get into animation and entertainment films.

Around this time, Dianne and John chose old friend Dennis Abey to direct the live action and Jonathan Peel to act for Penguin as executive producer. With similar alcohol tastes, the two have got on famously ever since. Jonathan went on to become MD of Millimages UK, and still is at time of writing.

To ensure quality, John, Dianne and Sally Floyer would walk around all three studios, at nine or 9.30 – a jaunt that Jonathan Peel nicknamed the conga. Sally was always late, so much so that the other members of the group eventually ran a book on betting what time she would get there. They started at Grand Slamm in Bloomsbury Street, then Stuart Brooks' studio in Charlotte Street, then up to TVC in Grafton Way and on to lunch in the Greek restaurant (The Glory, which gets a credit in *Granpa* – and Sally Floyer came to refer as The Gory!) As the BBC were going to buy them, Theresa Plummer Andrews, then head of BBC Children's co-productions and acquisitions, occasionally came on the congas to see what the studios were up to.

In addition to the conga, the production team had meetings upstairs at TVC and talked about the drawings and the scripts. "We used to argue for hours about the scripts", says Sally. "I made them change them because they weren't what the characters would say." A project like Beatrix Potter has

127

to look just right and Sally remembers a lot of arguments about what Peter Rabbit should look like, "There was Geoff Dunbar pinning up all these pictures against the wall and saying they're different, which one do you like?' And that was interesting and threw up a lot of inconsistencies."

More than the inevitable contentious moments, she remembers some of the more thrilling ones. "It was extremely exciting when we first saw the artwork. When Peter squeezed under the gate, turned around and tweaked his jacket. That was quite extraordinary as it wasn't in the original work, but you could see what the artists were trying to do. They were going to fill in the gaps." She also remembers one of Geoff's animators guiding her through an animated sequence: "he was talking the animation as he was doing it, actually visualising the action. They were almost being the character as they did it."

For John, the films were a tremendous success. "It was quite magical watching those films come together." It was very unusual as well, to have three films like that being shot at the same time, and certainly a departure from the normal production process. Most people were either making a half hour special or a series and needed it sequentially, but Penguin needed their films quickly.

Although everybody's brief was the same, the different studios' films all vary slightly. TVC's is more Snowman-esque, Grand Slamm was more commercial in lots of ways, and Stuart Brooks was more focused on the artwork and detail so their drawing was very involved. John was delighted overall with the studios and thought they had all done wonderfully well.

For the live action tops and tails, actress Niamh Cusack played Beatrix Potter and the Hilltop team did a week's location shoot in the Lake District. For the first series, they shot in the summer, when it was sunny. Series two was shot in late summer and autumn, where it rained the whole time. Regardless of the weather, the live-action shooting was great fun.

Dennis Abey proved as charismatic as ever throughout both shoots and always kept the mood light with his jokes and stories. John remembers introducing him to Sally Floyer: "Sally first met him at a little cocktail party, and he kept swearing as he usually does. She said, 'who's that

John Coates showcases Peter Rabbit drawing at the TVC studios. [© 2010 TV Cartoons Ltd.]

blaspheming man?' and I said he's our director of live action. 'Oh,' she said … anyway, later they got on like a house on fire, but only after I said he was in the Life Guards you know … I didn't tell her, he'd just been a dispatch rider."

Dennis had pulled all his usual crew from commercials for the shoot, and they also had on site the two children who voiced Peter and Benjamin so they could record the live action bits. John remembers they had their chaperone, a lady, with them. "On the last day of shooting, she asked her young charges, 'Have you had fun? Did you learn anything? And one of the children said yes, I learnt to whistle … and whistled. And she asked the other one, and did you learn anything. There was a pause and then the small boy piped up, "yes, I learnt to say cunt!'". Needless to say, the chaperone was speechless, and John and the rest of the crew cried with laughing.

There was also a contingent of Japanese at the shoot, representatives from Fuji Sankei, who were co-producers

129

on the films. John remembers a little mini-bus of them, all very polite and courteous. One time the TVC team and the Japanese had dinner and there was rabbit on the menu. Dianne (Jackson) was sitting next to John and dared him to order the rabbit, so he did, and so did she. It shocked everybody in the Japanese contingent. John remembers there was one really pretty Japanese girl who was also the most outgoing and who spoke the best English ... "Every morning, they'd all gather at the famous pub, The Tower Bank Arms, at 6 or 6.30 in the morning. The Japanese would trot up and bow, and after we got to know them really well, I said, you know all this bowing is polite, but we're in England now and here we kiss on the cheek. Oh, she said ... so the next morning, very formally, they all did it, so they all kissed ...".

The films were dancing along a pace but they still needed music. After talking to several composers, John and Dianne picked Colin Towns to write the Beatrix Potter score. "He proved to be a good choice because unlike many composers he actually got on with humanity rather well", says John. "It was no small feat to work with three different directors on six films and get on well with all of them."

The first film, *Peter Rabbit and Benjamin Bunny*, was broadcast on BBC 1 in the late afternoon and got an audience only just short of 10 million people, an amazing feat. The others didn't do quite as well but were all in the order of 7 or 8 million, which nowadays seems astonishing. They were a huge success and won prizes worldwide, including the 1993 BAFTA Nomination – Best Animation and the 1993 Emmy Award Nomination – Outstanding Animated Programme. Emmy aside, the films were a great hit in the US and John was pleased they had kept their original "English" voices.

The year after the first six films were delivered, they were aired in the US and John and Sally were invited on an 18 city radio tour of the nation, which was actually completely virtual: "We went to the top of a broadcasting building, somewhere in the middle of Manhattan, and had all these call in programmes", explains Sally. Their stint done, they would go off and have afternoon tea at the Plaza, which John enjoyed. The films got a lot of publicity because their release coincided with the 100 year anniversary of *The Tale of Peter Rabbit*: Beatrix Potter had written the tale of Peter Rabbit to a little boy in 1893 when he was in Scotland because he was ill. She didn't know what to say to him so she said she would tell him the tale of Peter Rabbit, and Penguin celebrated the anniversary of that letter in 1993.

For the first time ever, Peter Rabbit was being animated, quite a big thing since Beatrix Potter herself had turned down Disney in the thirties and no one had done anything since. Sally Floyer is more than happy with the result, commenting: "The films are very close to the original books, so 100 years on this is a good time to do it, to animate the Potter books, that was the message we were giving."

20

The Bump in the Road

John's working life was humming along fine; not only were his films garnering awards but so was he. In 1993 Theresa Plummer-Andrews presented him with a BBC Lifetime Achievement Award, which John refers to as his "old age" award. Theresa, still then head of BBC Children's Acquisitions, Co-productions, gave a small speech to mark the occasion. "He's made a few films here and there, but mostly, he's known as the man who put the L into lunch!" No one in the industry, and plenty outside of it, could argue with that!

While his professional life continued to zing along, things were not so great personally and, inevitably, John and Chris hit a bit of a sticky patch. During this period, he met a few nice ladies who he fondly remembers. In the September of 1993, while making the Beatrix Potter films, John attended the Cartoon Forum in Inverness. There, he reconnected with a young woman he had met some years previously at an animation seminar in Switzerland. He recalls back then being in a strange 1930s hotel at the Lake of Neuchatel where there was an extraordinary good-looking girl at the bar every evening. "I remember at the last evening I asked who she was. Anyway, a year or two later on my way to the Cartoon Forum at Inverness, I was enjoying a gin and tonic before catching the plane at Terminal 1, Heathrow. I was sitting at the top of a little spiral staircase that went up to the bar, when a fantastically good looking girl came over and kissed me on the cheek and said, you don't know who I am, do you? And it was her. "We travelled to Inverness together and that was lovely … and then an extraordinary thing happened on my return. There were two planes coming back, one was early so I avoided that, and caught the later one. There was an empty seat beside me and the whole plane went 'ohhh' when she came and sat in it! It was the only empty seat. How could she have had the seat reserved and held? I said how on earth did you manage that? She just giggled." Over time, they became good friends. Eurostar had just begun, and they would meet at the Musée d'Orsay. "I'd take the taxi at the Gare du Nord and then I'd have to find her amongst the animal sculptures outside the Musée."

A year or so later at another Cartoon Forum, John met another lady. "I got to know her at the forum in the Azores. Embarrassingly, I went over to her on the lawns where the bar was, and Jimmy Murakami was chatting to her. I went up and said I was lucky to say hello to the prettiest girl at the forum. We became friends and eventually she went to work for a company I was associated with."

On the subject of girls, John adds a note on the lovely PR doyen who looked after him at markets: "She became a very good friend, and looked after me at Mip and Mipcom and used to get my tickets for me at Cannes. To thank her, I would take her to lunch at one of the "posh" restaurants on the beach. I remember once she ordered a sea bass and it came whole and she went green. And a lady opposite said, "You can ask them to take the head off", you know. At the Cordoba Forum, John met another lady who he continues to enjoy lunches with, and still keeps in touch with a pretty girl he met at one of TVC's Christmas parties.

21

1995 – Three More Half Hour Specials

With the huge success of the first six Beatrix Potter episodes, it seemed to make sense to make another three films. Jumping Jack (Dave Unwin's company formed in the meantime) Geoff and Ginger and TVC did one each: *The Tale of the Flopsy Bunnies and Mrs. Tittlemouse*; *The Tale of Mr. Tod and the further Adventures of Peter Rabbit*; and the *Tale of Two Bad Mice and Johnny Town-Mouse*. They shot a new top and tail with Dennis Abey directing the live action, which worked out fine, despite the unceasing rain.

Peter Orton, of Hit fame, took over the distribution of the films and did fantastically well from them. In the US *The Tales of Beatrix Potter* became the favourite programme on television – and the video sales made him millions. The money he got from Beatrix Potter enabled him to go public: at that point, they'd sold something like 3 or 4 million videos in America at 19 or 20 dollars each, and Peter Orton took 35 per cent off the top.

TVC got a little bit of the profit in the end, but not an awful lot. Even so, there's an interesting little addendum to the story. After delivery of the first six, there was immediate talk of doing three more, but they kept being put off. TVC were running a bit low on funds and having quite a hard time – this was the time of recession and it had hit lots of independent studios in London. John had a decent share in the first six, around 25 per cent, so he offered Penguin the chance to buy back 5 per cent. Penguin said they would consider it, and produced an enormous sheet of facts and figures to prove that the films wouldn't be in profit until the year 2000 and something, and used that as an excuse for what John considered a real mean offer. He needed the money and didn't have much to bargain with, so Penguin upped the offer a tiny bit and then he accepted it. Stephen Hall was then the finance director, who the TVC team all liked and got on well with. John, incensed at their time schedule, told him "Stephen, I bet you £25,000 it's in profit by Christmas 1998. Ahaa, he said, it won't be. But I'll take you on." Time passed and then in November 1998, John came back from somewhere raising money and Norman was standing there grinning from ear to ear. "You won't guess but I've got a cheque here for £72,000.'" "I said what! And he said, Beatrix Potter went into profit in the September quarter and Stephen Hall has honoured the bet."

In the meantime, TVC had started on *Famous Fred*, based on the Posy Simmonds' book and directed by Joanna Quinn. With hindsight, John wishes he had not sold the share in the Beatrix Potter films now, but then it saved the day. "They were fun. Making them was fun."

The films are still distributed around the world, but now by BBC Worldwide, rather than Hit. John is unhappy with the decision which he sees no justification for, as Hit did so well with them. After an unsuccessful attempt at distributing the films themselves through a little distribution division, Penguin sold the rights to BBC Worldwide, which again doesn't sit easy with John. "The BBC Worldwide are alright, and the people there are awfully nice, but they don't have that feeling, they don't depend on selling the bloody things. Peter Orton did well. He was in business to make money."

John still thinks there is room to do another three films and make the nine into 12, though at the moment there is no sign of this happening. John still regrets that Penguin never got around to making the feature film. He admits there were some aspects in the feature Sally didn't like, which would have needed finding some level of agreement. Notably, there was a villain who she was not fond of, but, counters John, "a story called the adventures of Peter Rabbit needed more adventure than Mr McGregor's garden. TVC invented a wild dog running riot amongst the farm killing sheep. Sally was iffy about that. She didn't think it was true to Beatrix Potter, but you've got to enhance the whole thing or it's too limited for a feature."

22

The Wind in the Willows (1995) and The Willows in Winter (1996)

TVC started working on *The Wind in the Willows*, an animated version of Kenneth Grahame's classic tale while they were still working on the Beatrix Potter episodes. Ratty, Moley, and who can forget the irrepressible Toad, part of the famous riverbank set, John Coates had long wanted to do something with Kenneth Grahame's classic tale *The Wind in the Willows*, originally illustrated by Ernst Shepard. He got his chance after the success of the first six Beatrix Potter films when distributor Peter Orton took him to lunch and asked him what else he wanted to do. John didn't have to think twice: *The Wind in the Willows* had been in his sights for sometime. He started exploring the rights and discovered that story wise there was no problem, but he would have to go through the Shepard Estate if he wanted to use the original artwork. He tried that, but decided the publishers were a bit too "toffee nosed" about the whole thing and it would be better if TVC designed their own characters.

Peter Orton handled the finance side through Carlton, which had been newly organised. Carlton, for their part, were telling everybody what marvelous quality programmes they were going to make, including in their slate *The Wind in the Willows* and also *The Willows in Winter* – the original characters taken a stage further. John considered the latter an adventure story, but not very literary in many ways, but he and Dave Unwin, director of both films, met the Oxford-based author William Horwood anyway. Dave found him a no-nonsense type: "Before we started, he wanted to know who John was and everything, wanted to be reassured that everything would be of the highest quality. He came to the studio during the production and needed everything explained. He asked certain questions and was nobodies fool." It was all par for the course for John; he was used to working with all types of people and kept his eye on the prize – the film.

Peter Orton arranged the rights and Carlton pitched in with the money, which was quite high: the programmes were to be 75 minute, TV feature length, with a budget of £3 million each. There was a lot of development work to do, and while Penguin delayed the second three Beatrix Potter films, Carlton delayed *The Wind in the Willows*. It was a bad time for companies – international currency markets were all over the place, because of a dollar/pound crisis, and Carlton would not release the funding. It bit hard for TVC, then suffering from recession, as were many boutique operations at that time.

The news they were gearing up again came at quite an opportune time for John and his cohorts. Dennis Abey, who was going to direct the live action, had heard the L'Etoile restaurant was being reorganised and reopening on a certain Monday with Elena, who John and his gang had all followed around London for years and years. Dennis booked a table on the Friday, to give Elena a few days to settle down, and lunch was for John and Jonathan Peel, who was going to be executive producer on both films. They were sitting on the first table on the right of the restaurant and by all accounts enjoying a very good lunch and in no hurry to go anywhere, when the phone rang. It was Bella, John's PA, with the message Carlton had finally given the go ahead. John was unsure, and said: "Oh go on Bella, we've had that every Friday", but she insisted, 'No, it's the real thing this time". She convinced him anyway and they left about half past 6, hardly able to stand up. To this day, the table is known as the £3 million table because of the budget: "We drank a

whole bottle of Calvados and ordered another bottle of Champagne, one of those nicely painted bottles. I've still got that painted bottle in my office. And it was true. They were ready to go at last."

Voices provided by Left to Right, Michael Palin (Rat) Michael Gambon (Badger) Rik Mayall (Toad) and Alan Bennett (Mole). [© Carlton UK TV 1995.]

It was great to get the green light, but Carlton still wanted the same deadline, even though the delay had been at their end and they had admitted it. This put Dave Unwin under huge stress; even without the delay, the pressure was on – *The Wind in the Willows* was for Christmas 1995 and *The Willows in Winter*, Christmas 1996 – but the late start made it infinitely worse. They had to hit the ground running on what was a huge film, 75 minutes in total, including 56 minutes of animation. Dennis Abey shot the live action sequences for both on the Thames, the first at Eton and the second near Oxford. Despite the pressures at the studio, all had a good time for these top and tail sequences. For the first shoot it was sunny. For the second, it rained.

Vanessa Redgrave as Narrator was part of a stellar line up for the voices put together by casting director Celestia Fox: Alan Bennett was Mole, Michael Gambon, Badger, Rik Mayall, Toad and Michael Palin, Ratty. John hugely enjoyed the voice recordings, which were done at George Martin's studios up in Hampstead. He got to have afternoon tea with Alan Bennett: they chatted about this and that. And sometimes George, who knew them all, would come down when they broke at six o clock with a bottle of wine.

The operational hub for the animation was a production studio in Whitfield Street, just around the corner from Grafton Way. It was a nice big, open area to put rows of tracers and painters, with a semi-computerised editing system, as John puts it, "a concoction put together by our 'mad editor', Taylor Grant."

The TVC team had to do storyboards and all the pre-production before they could actually start, so they were always short of time. Production went well, considering they had lost months and months of production time waiting for the green light, but there was serious falling out between John and TVC over Carlton's handing of the whole thing. TVC had to work around the clock at the end, to make up for lost time because of the late start. They went into massive overtime to get the film delivered, says John and Carlton were adamant they would sort everything out – TVC's job was just to deliver the film, which was booked for Christmas afternoon. John did deliver as promised.

As one film was a classic and the other a sequel, the two films were treated differently. With the first, *The Wind in the Willows*, "there was this sense we had to be very respectful", explains Dave, who thinks because of that the film was perhaps a bit more worthy than it might have been otherwise.

Earlier, Cosgrove Hall had done a model version with David Jason as the main voice and concentrating on the funny bits. In the TVC version, John, Dave and Ted, the writer, took the decision to take it "warts and all", even going against Carlton sometimes to get their own way. Part of the matter was the style of the book, written in Edwardian times and a

because he has no idea of style, he tends to look rather overdressed.
I was insistent that the characters should be animals, not human
beings with animal heads.

"Badger is probably a retired Headmaster - his clothes are
old and patched and he's broken down the backs of his slippers.
Mole is a particularly round and cuddly creature and actually quite
a sharp-toothed young gentleman, and Ratty is the quintessential
Englishman."

The feel and colouring of the film comes from the Art
Director Loraine Marshall who also worked on Granpa
and Father Christmas.

"I take over the line drawings that the animators do
and turn everything into colour, and have to decide on the
spot whether Mole's teeth should be more yellow or white!"
Says Loraine "I wanted a sort of soft feel to the film because
there's lots of landscapes and countryside - so we thought
we'd go that way rather than a cartoon style."

TVC founder John Coates and
executive producer Jonathan Peel

bit fey nowadays, especially with the Shepard illustrations. As Dave Unwin points out, "the great god Pan is a bit of a classical wuss, without any of the elemental power". Anyway, Carlton wanted to do away with the great god Pan sequence, saying it was embarrassing and no one would want to watch it. John and Dave argued that it was essential because it linked into Ratty on the river and crystalised the whole thing, the underlying power of nature. So there was no choice, they had to do it. Carlton didn't want to, recalls Dave, "and John said, 'well, we are,' and we did …".

At the time *The Willows in Winter* started, Carlton were not John's favourite people; he makes no bones about the fact there was a lot of bad feeling towards the company. Even so, TVC's hard work had produced an excellent quality film, which garnered art director Loraine Marshall a primetime Emmy. "We worked so hard. Loraine was in tears in the end. It was a real nightmare", explains John. Still the team had to deliver and get on with the next one. Given the second film was not the revered classic, TVC didn't have to be so mindful of what they were dealing with and could use a bit of artistic license. In this film, Toad falls in love with a biplane and despite all his vehement promises never to get

Excerpt from Carlton/ TVC brochure, showing Jonathan Peel, executive producer, and John Coates. [© Carlton UK TV 1995.]

140

obsessed with machines again, Toad the consummate narcissist is soon at it again, and up, up and away in his new flying machine.

"We put in more jokes, more fun", says Dave, "and for me that makes the film more watchable. Also, where *The Wind in the Willows* was written as more of a mishmash, with lots of separate stories, some of which join up and some do not, *The Willows in Winter* is a clear narrative so in some ways was easier to adapt". Not to forget, the team had also learnt a lot, especially how to move the characters. They understood them, which really helped to effectively translate them on screen. John agrees that the second film has the edge over the first: "If one was really honest, that was the better film because (a) we had the proper time to make it, and (b) it was quite a strong story, adventure wise. Toad's in his airplane and dive-bombs this bridge, animated but copied from the bridge used in the live action shoot."

The Willows in Winter was hampered by production problems, and not of TVC's making. It should not have really turned out like that; after all the team were already ahead of the game – they had finished *The Wind in the Willows* and all the characters, many of the sets, etc, were already done. Unfortunately, Warner Bros opened up a studio in Covent Garden, London, and were paying massive money, and that hit TVC hard. Dave recalls, "we lost 15 animators in a week and several other staff. The guy who was our runner went to work at Warners for more money than we were paying our animators. It was outrageous really and totally skewed the market in the UK." Suddenly, TVC were short of crew, and this happened to be a period when Warners were employing large numbers of people. "There was a lot of work in London generally, but we struggled just because we didn't have enough workers. We got over it but we lost time. It happens", says Dave. To keep-up staff moral, Richard Nye, SFX director on the film, designed little badges that stated: "I haven't been asked to work at Warner Brothers".

John managed to keep calm under the pressure and rally his staff in the process. Erica Darby, then a checker on the film who now has her own studio, Spider Eye, recalls: "We were really behind schedule and a lot of animation was being sent back to be redone, at a point when we didn't have time to

do it. We were doing a lot of hours but not making any ground." The problem was explained during a production meeting upstairs and John said he would write a communication from the Producer, urging everyone to keep up the effort. "The next morning each of us had stuck on the doors of our rooms a notice bearing the legendary 'NO FUSS-POTTING'. In capitals like that, so it did seem important, but that was the entire communication. I don't know if it's documented whether or not we made up any time after that, but the film did get delivered in time for its airdate! What I particularly like about it is it was on all of our doors, no fingers pointed!"

Dave Unwin, who directed both films, with some sketches of Toad. [© Carlton UK TV 1995.]

In the end, to get around the problem, TVC sent some work to Ireland and some work to a Hungary, at Varga Studios. At the end of it, John invited a lot of Varga people over to The Curzon for the charity premiere. It's not ideal working with people outside the UK, because you're playing on the back foot, says Dave Unwin. "It's fire brigade work rather than something that was planned from the start, which always tends to be difficult. But there you are, that was the situation we were in and that's how we got out of it."

Despite the difficulties making the film, Dave enjoyed

working with John. "Some producers don't have a clear idea of what they are looking for and that means that getting the result they want is difficult. John always knows what he wants and that makes him great to work with."

Years after production, John is still proud of both films, and believes they stand the test of time. TVC's film was first broadcast on Christmas Day 1995 and went on to collect a Special Jury Prize at the Rockie Awards as well as the aforementioned Prime Time Emmy for its art direction.

By the time *The Wind in the Willows* and *The Willows in Winter* finished, John was in his mid 60s and showing no signs of slowing down. If anything, starting producing somewhat later in life seemed to galvanise him, perhaps more so than younger producers. In a fast moving world, the quality of his films shone through. Typically, John took time from his busy schedule to visit his beloved Provence, France. When he wasn't working, he could invariably be found on the shores of the Lac de Sainte Croix in Aguine, where he loves to swim.

23

Famous Fred

John stayed close to his sister Anne but that didn't stop him enjoying a friendly rivalry with her. Anne had won an Oscar in 1963 for editing the David Lean epic *Lawrence of Arabia* and John coveted an Oscar on his mantelpiece, even if it was just to rival his sister.

Having failed with *The Snowman*, he got another chance in 1996 when he started on *Famous Fred*, mid way through the production of the Beatrix Potter series and *The Wind in the Willows, The Willows in Winter*. 'Fred' is the eponymous dead cat in Posy Simmonds' book. Published in 1987, she was moved to write the story following the death of a young friend. There were many cats where she was living at the time, so she combined the two things to come up with the story of a family moggy, posthumously revealed to be the iconic rock star, Famous Fred.

It was publisher Tom Maschler, at Jonathan Cape, who bought Posy's book to John Coates' attention: Tom had previously put John on to *Granpa*, so when he said he had something else that was interesting, John listened. At the time, TVC were in the middle of the Beatrix Potter films but John loved Posy's book and after some pretty-intense negotiations with her agent, finally got the rights. "We were hard bargained."

The rights secured, John needed a director. Both he and Dianne Jackson were big fans of Joanna Quinn's work so, as Dianne's health was deteriorating, she chose to be supervising director and Joanna to direct the film. John recalls: "We all met with Posy and discussed how it (the film) should go, and we all laughed because the first words in the book come from the two children, 'Our cat Fred is

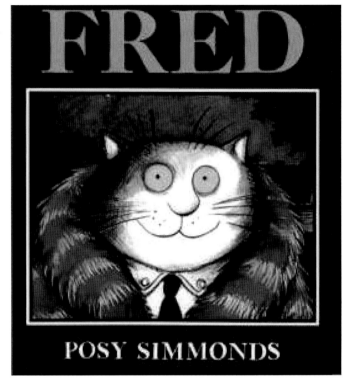

dead'. Dealing with death was perfect for TVC who joked about how they had done in many of their lead characters, quips John: "We melted the snowman, killed off Jim and Hilda, did in Grandpa and now with Fred we got the death bit over at the beginning ...".

Posy's first image of the book was a cat dressed as an undertaker, and the film opens with brother and sister Sophie and Nick grieving for the loss of their pet cat, Fred. All is sad and maudlin until the sound of a cats' chorus breaks through the cold night air and the children begin to realise that their hearth-loving ginger Tom had a whole other side to him. In the film, Kenneth the hamster's wondrous tales of Fred's ballyhoo alter ego lift the children's sadness; they realise that Fred was indeed a rock star and there was no need to weep for him. Kenneth delights in his story-telling, like the time the children thought their pets were missing, they were really on a world tour, taking in the Las Vegas hot spots and indulging in all kinds of tom-cat-foolery.

Posy was thrilled at the prospect of TVC turning her book into a film, especially a musical ... She had heard from fellow Jonathan Cape authors, John Burningham and Raymond Briggs, that John was great to work with and wanted to find out for herself. She remembers several great lunches at L'Etoile to discuss how the film was going to pan out. The book was already close to perfect for a film adaptation but John felt it needed another character, a narrator. He materialised in the form of Kenneth the guinea pig, who Posy says she invented because: "I thought he would have lovely little fingers and be able to sew sequins on Fred's costume, which was very important". In addition, a guinea pig would be in the house, which bought another dimension to the film. There is also a nice in-joke in the movie. Kenneth, the guinea pig is Fred's dresser and Tom Courtenay did the voice of Kenneth, and he had been in the film *The Dresser*. "He was wonderful", says Posy. It might have been another Tom, none other than Tom Jones, the erstwhile "Welsh Elvis", for the voice of Fred. His people had been sent the script and were interested because of the song, "What's new Pussycat", but when they found out Fred was actually dead, they turned it down – they didn't want Tom Jones to be a dead cat. Lenny Henry didn't have the same concerns and happily did the voice of Fred.

The film had obvious commercial appeal so the money angle worked out relatively straight forward. John approached his heroes, Channel 4, who found the idea of another John Coates half-hour attractive and put up £500k, half the budget. Joanna Quinn was already an admired animator/director and as she worked in Wales and had the support of Welsh C4 – S4C, there was a possibility S4C would co-produce the film. TVC were heavily tied up with the Beatrix Potter production at the time and John needed a good line producer for "Fred". He figured Catrin Unwin, wife of TVC stalwart Dave Unwin, would be perfect for the role: not only did she speak Welsh, but she also lived within driving distance of Joanna's studio – so it would be like a normal daily job. John went to see S4C in Cardiff to see if they would put any money into it. He recalls it was one of "those funny meetings where I think, rudely, they spoke Welsh. The joke was, they didn't even know that Catrin was Welsh, and they were starting to talk among themselves ... and Catrin chirped up in Welsh, and the look on their faces."

S4C put in 200k and eventually, and SCI – I for international – put in another 100k. John was still missing 200k: "I tried as hard as I could, and couldn't get Channel 4 to put any more in and getting the video people to invest wasn't then part of the normal scene. Things came to a point where we couldn't raise any more." During this time, which was about 5 years, C4 said they couldn't leave the money sitting there and gave John just three months to raise the rest of it. Luckily, TVC was prospering as a company: *The Snowman* was starting to bring in impressive funding and was doing well. John decided to bite the bullet: "I suddenly thought at the next meeting why don't I say, TVC will put 200k in and get us a bigger share – I didn't think anyone was going to check my bank to see I hadn't got 200k lying about. Next meeting everybody said, yes, great! All agreed and obviously meant it. The people investing were putting their money in and we always seemed to have enough to pay the bills."

Having finally got the go ahead to make the film, TVC didn't have enough animators to work on the film. There was an army of animators in London but they were all working on *The Wind in the Willows* and could not be spared. There weren't many animators in Wales, and Joanna had already seconded any that were available to work on the film. Fortunately, she had a house and contacts in Spain so she and John decided to go to Madrid and see if they could raise a couple of animators there. John had a friend who used to be with Studio Moro, since closed down. Moro put together a little Spanish unit and Joanna picked two or three animators from that; they did quite a lot of it in the end, and rather well, John reckons.

When *Famous Fred* was finished and nominated for an Oscar, "S4C went to town with the publicity and took real liberties", says John. The contractual wording of the film was a TVC London production for Channel 4 and S4C, which on their publicity became a TVC Cardiff production for S4C and Channel 4, without asking either party.

Worse, John considered S4C had treated Joanna shabbily and that made his blood boil. "When we finally arrived in Hollywood the whole of S4C came and they flew Joanna and her boyfriend in the back of the plane, and S4C bosses all went first class. John recalls, "The publicity man was quite fun, he was very tongue in cheek about it all. We were

147

all standing outside the hotel they were staying in. I said to the publicity man you have got something behind your back, and he looked at me very sheepishly. It was a Welsh flag. We allowed them one picture with it and that was their lot."

The Oscar-nominated team. Left to right. Joanna Quinn, Nigel Crowle (lyricist), John Coates, Paul Madden, Catrin Unwin, Norman Kauffman, Richard Nye. [© 2010 TV Cartoons Ltd.] Fred as kitten [© 2010 TV Cartoons Ltd./S4C]

Posy was delighted with the finished product. "I thought they had caught the quality of the book, and lots of things were straight out of it; and then the inserts of adult parties, I think Joanna had obviously studied my *Guardian* grown ups that I do in the paper so they were all there too. The ending of the film is different from the book. In the book, Fred died, but in the film he has nine lives, which Posy was unsure about at first: "that was the only bit I wondered, that I had made him actually dead. But I accepted it. I think in the book it was important he was dead but in the film not so much."

Famous Fred didn't win an Oscar, so John still has to catch up with Anne on that score, but remains a wonderfully popular film and was awarded the Grand Prix for Best Animated TV Program (Series or Special) at the 1997 Annecy Animated Film Festival.

It also won the best children's award at BAFTA in 1996, which added to John's glittering list of prizes, and John was awarded yet another life time achievement award, also from BAFTA in 1996.

John was almost 70 by now and had seen many changes in the world and in his own life. Politically, England was ripe for something new, and saw hope in the enthusiastic leader of the Labour Party, Tony Blair. After years in opposition, Labour won the General Election of 1997 ending their 'Wilderness years'. Now it was all about Blair, who won by a landslide – 418 seats. That same year, Princess Diana died in a car crash in France, and there was a national outpouring of grief in England the like of which has never been seen before or since.

24

The Bear

B y the time John came to make his next film, *The Bear*, he was 71, but still with the energy and zest for life of a much younger man. At home, John and Chris had weathered the storm, and were still together. His youngest daughter Giulietta was making a name for herself as an artist, though sadly, for her sister Nicola, Adam's illness meant she had to focus on keeping an income stream for the family and had to abandon her own plans for a company. John's grandchildren were then at school, Ben was 10 and Clio, 7, and John wondered what kind of world they would find when they became adults.

Meanwhile, in the literary world, a new wizard had arrived – *Harry Potter and the Philosopher's Stone* was to become a massive global hit that saw author J.K. Rowling's earnings propelled into the stratosphere. Not that her books impacted on John; he has never been given to fads and carried on picking projects as he always had – the ones that made the hairs on his neck stand up, the ones that he felt had the power to move and entertain.

Such a project was *The Bear* (1998). Creatively breathtaking, *The Bear* never moved the critics as *The Snowman* had done, simply because they considered it to be a sequel to the latter, and therefore nothing new.

"If *The Snowman* had never happened, *The Bear* would have been a huge success", suggests Howard Blake, who composed and orchestrated the music for the film as he had for *The Snowman* some 20 years earlier. *The Bear* might well carry a strong ecological message, but no one seems to care. If *The Snowman* came out to a fanfare, *The Bear* shuffled apologetically on stage – there wasn't even a premier. For all

The Bear. *Original book cover of Raymond Briggs'* The Bear. *[© 2010 Jonathan Cape Ltd.]*

its award-winning excellence,* *The Bear* can only ever seem like a poor relation to *The Snowman*.

Years before, after *The Snowman*, Channel 4 executives had asked for such a follow-up. After all, a "Snowman II" was out of the question: the snowman had melted, and that was not about to change – Raymond and John were both adamant about that. At the time, John was winding down TVC's own animation studio, so this last film was the end of an era. *The Bear* was meant as *The Snowman* sequel to bring TVC a full 360°.

The Bear's simple strong message ripples through the beautiful animation: wild animals, like this Bear, should not be in cages, but free in the wild. Like *The Snowman*, this is a transcendence film, this time with a little girl, Tilly, who

* *The Bear* won several Grand Prix and heaps of other awards, including a Peabody Award for Excellence.

drops her teddy bear in the polar bear pit during a day out at London zoo. Later that night, the same polar bear appears in her bedroom, with the little girl's very own teddy bear and takes her on a moonlight odyssey in the crisp London night, skating along the Thames, then finally up into the sky where he introduces her to Ursa Major – the spirit of the Great Bear.

The Coates–Briggs relationship having withstood the test of time, and three previous films, the agreement for *The Bear* was straightforward; a gentleman's agreement no doubt forged in a local pub near Raymond's Sussex home – he hates coming up to London. After that, John took the book to show Clare Kitson, who commissioned the film on the spot. She agreed that the book was magical and loved the ecological message. There were discussions as to whether the story was too similar to *The Snowman* but an informal survey of children's classics established that as the same theme of friendship and loss was at the core of a great many books, *The Bear* would be in good company: "I didn't have to think about it because that was one of the few genres I didn't have to battle with the channel for. They knew periodically they would want a half hour special. Like me, they trusted John implicitly." Having given the nod, Channel 4 found some development money and was prepared to give half the budget, which was half of 1.2 million. In the middle of this, Miramax and Harvey Weinstein got involved. Apparently, his wife was interested in animation, so he contacted Colin Leventhal, then a senior exec at C4 and long time supporter of TVC. Colin sent him the animatic of the whole film of *The Bear*, which was 26 minutes of drawn pictures with no track. The film must have hit the spot because not long afterwards, and to John's delight, Harvey offered $1.5 million for world rights. Colin upped him a bit, to $1.6 and world rights, except UK, and Harvey agreed. *The Bear* was in production before they could blink.

For John, *The Bear* was a chance to bring together a lot of people he had worked with over the years: "I have to say it was really quite a happy and uncomplicated production: the people who had started on *The Snowman* years before had become pretty professional and knew exactly how to put the whole thing together. Ian McCue, line producing, Richard Nye, for the special effects, which were very important in

Clare Kitson, who commissioned The Bear, *with John Coates, in Tel Aviv. [© 2010 TV Cartoons Ltd.]*

that film with the star bear: There was a great team of people and off we went. The end result was remarkable.

It was fitting *The Bear* was meant as a sequel to *The Snowman*, because John wanted to reunite the original '*Snowman*' team to make it, with the exception of Dianne Jackson who had died tragically young some years previously. "I always knew I was going to get Hilary (Ardus) to direct it and Jo Jo Harrison (formerly Fryer) as art director and never regretted my choice." From there, the drill was the same, to work up a treatment based on the book for a half hour special. They did, which meant changing the story line to fit the TV timeline: the star bear fantasy isn't in the book at all, and the trip down through London and skating on the frozen Thames was all TVC.

Like *The Snowman*, the story in Raymond's book had to be expanded to make a film. Hilary and Jo Jo developed the star bear after one night brainstorming. Hilary had spent the night at Jo Jo's and, as they didn't have a spare room, had slept in her daughter's room, at the time covered in luminous stars and planets. This inspired Hilary who then thought of Ursa Major, the Great Bear as the star bear. Like others in the industry, Hilary, who had started with TVC in 1973 as a trainee assistant animator, acknowledges the strength of John's light touch. "He does involve himself up to a point, but then he doesn't interfere. He lets the director get on with what they are doing. He doesn't meddle but then on the other hand, where there is a crisis or something, he does jump in and take people out to lunch and have a quiet word. And of course, he knows how to raise money."

The old TVC guard fitted together well, but animating *The Bear* had its own problems, notably many painters and tracers had been retired because of the Animo computer paint system. Hilary managed to get Sarah Markham, who had worked at TVC before and had a team of people in Wales. Even so, they were below par: they couldn't paint flat. Renderers had become a victim of their own success; they had got the technique down off pat but the effect was too airbrushed. They had lost the scribbled feel, which made *The Snowman* and *Father Christmas* and *Granpa* so special. Hilary felt they needed to loosen up a bit. The look was lost as they got more perfectionist.

Richard Nye's special effects for the star bear were the hardest part of the shoot and took a lot of time and many tests. It was complicated because there were so many dope sheets. "There were an insane amounts of runs under camera because of all the star effects, so it took a long time to shoot: a four second scene could take three days to shoot. Even then, things could go wrong and sometimes did", says Hilary Ardus. Luckily, John was patient as ever, even when there was no choice but to stick the thing back under camera and shoot it again.

In the middle of production, broadcasters switched over to widescreen format, so the team had to adapt the film to the new size, which, luckily, turned out to be not too complicated. Most of the action was in the middle, so it was a matter sometimes of adding a tree in the corner of the frame if it looked empty.

Look closely and you'll see representations of the key members dotted throughout the film. Hilary Ardus (director) is the woman selling snow globes, Joanna Harrison (art director) is seen at the zoo with her family, Paul Madden (executive producer) is the sailor who spots the little bear on the ice-flow. In the night flight, author Raymond Briggs is the smiling face of the man in the moon; John Coates is the baby in the cot, and has a JC on his baby grow, composer Howard Blake is the pianist at the window and the film Tilly and her family watch on TV is *The Snowman*.

Like *The Snowman*, *The Bear* is wordless, apart from the lyrics

The star bear was very difficult to animate but Richard Nye makes the finished work look effortless.
[© 2010 TV Cartoons Ltd.]

in the one song, *Somewhere a Star Shines for Everyone*. It was hard to find the right girl singer for the piece, but eventually, after a bit of trial and error, a new girl appeared on the scene that was perfect for the job. Her name was Charlotte Church, who went on to become a star in her own right. To represent the bears, Howard used a tenor for the polar bear and a bass-baritone for the star bear.

The film went smoothly from inception through production and working with Harvey Weinstein and Miramax, which John was tenuous about, turned out to be fine. Everybody loved the film. Harvey Weinstein wrote John the most amazing note saying how lovely it was and called up Howard to say the same. In fact the film turned out to be a surprisingly easy experience for John, who had feared Harvey might want to take over the thing. "He never did. He loved the film", says John.

For the US market, TVC had to put a commentary for American children, as when Miramax did a test screening they could not follow the story. It irked John they asked for a commentary: "They talked about getting Julia Roberts to read it and they sent us several versions, all of which were awful, real American cutesy stuff. I refused, and I was in a position luckily. They persisted and sent someone over to talk to me. I said, I'm not totally against it, if that's going to make a big difference to sales in America." Some time later, John heard that Harvey Weinstein had met Judi Dench and liked her, so he asked if they could use her. John said yes but only if he liked the script. They sent one that was pretty good and TVC simplified it, and sent word it would be ok.

154

They went ahead and recorded with Judi Dench, who did the job beautifully. "I had to give in and that went out in America", says John. "Unfortunately, *The Bear* is hardly seen these days – it is part of the huge Miramax library and doesn't seem to get the airplay it surely merits. Channel 4 screens it most years and it continues to get a good audience. The Miramax library is now part of Disney. I think perhaps if it went into profit we might hear back, but it's all rather too complicated and boring."

The final film is certainly powerfully reminiscent of *The Snowman*, a little bit too much for Raymond's liking: "I was slightly annoyed they made it too like the sequel to *The Snowman*. In the book, there's nothing about Christmas, nothing about snow. The bear does leave footprints when he leaves but that's just convenience to show he's gone. But that (snow) is what the market wanted."

Acknowledging that the TVC team had to extend the book, which wasn't dramatic enough for an animated half-hour, nonetheless he doesn't see why the film had to be silent. "There's quite a lot of good dialogue in the book, I think, the editor thought so as well. I thought the book was quite funny, the way Tilly talks to the bear, all that kind of thing. But it had to be a silent film to make it look like *The Snowman!*"

After *The Bear*, John hit a bit of a wall. Professionally, he had achieved success many could only dream of. There was no shortage of work and his reputation was such that he could have gone on cherry picking the best projects for TVC. But he was in something of a quandary, what was next, he wondered.

25

Bali – Another Exotic Holiday

He figured a change of air and of scene would help him make his mind up and decided to take a holiday. He wanted somewhere hot and exotic and chose Bali, where he had always wanted to visit. John and Chris flew Singapore Airlines to Singapore, where they spent a night, and found by sheer chance they were in a hotel where TVC had made a one minute commercial to launch it internationally. Strange, indeed! John recalls how they, "went up in these amazing glass lifts, all of which we'd done in animation …".

Next morning, they flew on to Bali and then to the hotel, not knowing much about it. John quickly realised they weren't very far from the airport; in fact he thought they were too near the airport, although actually it wasn't overly noisy. The hotel turned out to be French owned and served the best croissants John has ever tasted – even though he owns a house in Provence. It was an exclusive place where no expense was spared on guests. For breakfast, John and Chris had their own garden and their own fountain, captivating both of them. On site, there was a big Indonesian restaurant and also there was a small French restaurant, with flaming torches, on the beach, which was really romantic. John and Chris got to know the manager there. All in all the people were charming, though John wasn't taken with Bali at all, apart from the hotel, which he found gorgeous.

After a while, John and Chris felt they weren't doing much, so they went to the Four Seasons, the posh bar, for a gin and tonic before lunch. It was quite a walk from their hotel and he enjoyed the brisk exercise. Overall, it was a great holiday, although there were all sorts of rules and regulations about driving there. "If you had an accident it was your fault immediately and the police put you in jail or put you in the police station", says John. He wasn't having any of that so he hired a driver and did a tour up to the volcanoes. He was disappointed to find at the summit it was packed with people, just packed. "It was crazy. There about 5 million Australians, and every time you stopped to look at something, there were thousands of people looking at the same thing."

Being involved in a mad crush wasn't John or Chris's idea of fun so they scuttled back and stayed in their hotel, which was luxurious by any standards. Later, they did escape the throng enough to have a few adventures, including a catamaran trip down the coast. The two young boys who owned it were quite taken with Chris, John recalls, "we fished first, and caught some funny little different fish … And then they said, "we're taking you down there and there's a little village". We went in with our fish and the elderly old lady, who ran a kind of a restaurant where you sat on the floor. She cooked the fish, and we had this amazing meal, surrounded by surfers, South American, all covered in that red ointment where they cut themselves on the coral. They were all in hammocks, living there with their girls. "It was rather a strange life", muses John, "living in a druggy haze most of the time … The fish were lovely with rice and salad, but I didn't catch them. Chris did. Typical, she would bloody catch them!"

26

John Winds Up TVC's Animation Studio

The *Bear* was to be TVC studio's last produced film; John had thought several years earlier that it was time to wind up TVC's production facility and had mulled over all the ramifications in Bali. The studio was 40 years old and he was getting on into his 70s and wanted a new direction. He made the final decision to wind things down at Mipcom, after he had presented a storyboard for his next planned film, *Oi Get Off Our Train*, to Colin Rose, then with the BBC. Colin had invited him for a very expensive lunch at Eden Rock – Hotel du Cap. John remembers pulling up at this fabulous hotel in his hired little Fiat Punto, and still recalls the diffident look on the valet's face as he went to park it – it seemed everyone else had a Rolls Royce or something suitably flashy. The two men met up and spent an hour going through the storyboard, and then they walked down the pretty gravel path, where all the film stars go, to the restaurant hanging over the rocks to the millionaires yachts below and had lunch, which was delicious, and far from pretentious.

When he was finished, in the late afternoon, he was all set to drive back to the "bunker" as the basement floor of the Mipcom exhibition hall is called. The same valet brought his car to the front door of the hotel for him, with the same diffident air. John sped off and, in some kind of peculiar instance he can not explain, thought he didn't want to go

John winds up TVC as a production studio. TVC continued as a production company but closed its own studio, much to the despair of the crew who loved to work there. TVC had been such a fixture in Soho for so long, no one really believed John when he said he was shutting up shop. This trunk (above) was used as a change of address card.
[© 2010 TV Cartoons Ltd.]

back to that "boring bunker" with all those people talking about "stuff". Having achieved so much, he wondered what next – what was he going to do with his life now?

Below: Image to celebrate TVC's 45th Happy Birthday.
[© 2010 TV Cartoons Ltd.]

After he had gone a few miles, he decided to go back to his hotel in Mougins, pack his bags and head off to who knows where. That evening, he headed off up to the area where he now has a house. He went to The Bastide hotel in Tourtour,

which claims to be France's prettiest village. They had a room so he stayed the night, and then decided to zigzag up France. He had a hire car that he presumed could be delivered anywhere and thought he would slowly head up to Paris and fly back to England from there. He spent three days thinking about life and staying in little favourite places.

Abracadabra (1980) montage showing TVC films and advertisements over the years.
[©2010 TV Cartoons Ltd./John Coates.]

He didn't book anywhere, but was lucky and got a room everywhere he went. The weather was incredible, brilliant sunshine – it was early October and it was a very special run. When he arrived back at the studio, his mind was made up – he was going to give everyone two years notice and would wind the whole thing up. After that, he was not sure what he was going to do. True to his word, he did give everyone two years notice, although no one at TVC believed he was going to go through with it, until some two years later when the redundancy packages were handed out. John and the TVC crew had a farewell lunch: all the staff received two years redundancy pay so they were all laughing and they all stayed on until the bitter end. The company had a last supper, fittingly, at L'Etoile. They were 13.

27

Oi Get Off Our Train and Varga TVC – 1998

lthough TVC as an animation studio was to all intents and purposes defunct, the company still produced another film called *Oi Get Off Our Train* via a co-production with Varga. John Burningham, author of *Granpa*, had been asked to do an exposition in Japan, at the Osaka World Fair, to showcase the first imported Japanese Railway locomotive. The organisers commissioned him to write a book, the only stipulation being it had to incorporate the engine. He came up with *Oi Get off Our Train*, a book with a strong ecological message. In the book, a small boy goes to bed and dreams that he and his stuffed dog, now a railroad engineer, are speeding through the night playing games and picking up endangered animals. Each animal that gets on board is told in no uncertain terms, *Oi Get Off Our Train*, and has to give a reason why they do not have to – the elephant because someone wants to cut off its tusks, the stork because the marshland where it lives is being drained and so on ... .

The organisers wanted an animation short to run actually in the station at either end of the trip for waiting passengers, and that is where TVC came in. *Dream Express* was the name of the short and John (Burningham) chose to work with TVC on the project because of his great experience working with them on *Granpa*. The film came together well and was

a big success, so much so that John wanted to make a longer version. He hoped that the Japanese Railway would pay for a half-hour special, but they didn't. John eventually raised the money for a half-hour through the BBC, especially Colin Rose at BBC Bristol and ZDF who were very involved in getting it off the ground. Jimmy Murakami was going to direct the film.

In the meantime, Varga had approached John with the offer of a merger. In theory, it seemed a sensible idea; he could go on living in his office and they would hire a lot of ex-TVC staff into the bargain. They had all the painting, computers in Budapest that could do all of that work, which he didn't have and was going to have to learn to do and get involved in. This seemed the better solution, a tidy arrangement that everybody felt good about.

The head of Varga, Andras Erkel, became executive producer on the film. It was done through the office they had opened up in the TVC building and called itself Varga TVC. The merger started promisingly enough: but it quickly deteriorated. The whole thing broke up and Varga moved out and John got his building done up in the process, which he sold for a million fairly soon afterwards. "That was the best thing about it: I got my building painted."

Creatively, the only good thing to come out of the TVC Varga experiment, says John, was *Oi Get Off Our Train*, which he thinks works quite well because Varga didn't interfere with it. It was a 50/50 venture, but TVC made it really, although Andreas did the trace and paint with his then new computers. "It's a nice little film", says John. "The

163

Image from the book; John Burningham used a scratchy style, similar to Granpa. [© 2010 Random House.]

budget was about half my usual budget. Much nicer than half the films that are around now …". The BBC has the rights these days, though the contract resides with Varga. "I could see it, but they can't find it. I find dealing with the BBC never gets you anywhere."

John would like to get the film re-released if possible, even though in a sense it belongs to Varga and not to him. "It was never actually shown around the world and that is a shame because it is a very charming film. Varga closed so it is difficult to find appropriate information now. Children's audiences have seen it and loved it. BBC did very little with it in the end, and considering the rubbish they broadcast I'm really surprised they haven't taken advantage of all the runs they had on it. Anyway, you never know."

Scene from the film with the boy and his dog. [© 2010 Varga/TV Cartoons Ltd./John Burningham.]

28

John's Brothers

ike her youngest brother, John's illustrious sister Anne has made her life in media and film. Not so, John's two elder brothers, Michael and David, who chose very different life-paths.

Michael was the eldest by about two years, then David, and then after quite a long gap of some years, came Anne, who was two years older than John. Both John's brothers went into the forces but embarked on very different life-paths. Michael went into North West Europe and was Captain Coates up until the end of the war. David went into the RAF, but he didn't want to be commissioned and ended up having the laziest life according to John. "He was on the coast in Kenya for most of the war – don't know whether it was radar, searching for aircraft and submarines during the whole of the Japanese time and never did anything amazing or brave, as he admitted when he got back. He had a really nice time, better than us being doodle bugged." After the war, Michael had fallen in love with the local farmers wife, Kay, a Czech girl who had two daughters, and additionally they had a daughter of their own called Gay. He bought an open Delage, the French equivalent of a Bentley with a strap down bonnet and no hood, and set off with Kay and the three kids for the south of France, not knowing exactly what they were doing. Fortunately, Michael had money from his pension at the end of the war, and they went and settled in Cagnes-Sur-Mer, between Nice and Cannes. It was an old town and already had an established artists colony, and that's where he settled and painted. He sold some paintings. He married Kay and lived there for quite some years.

Eventually, the marriage broke up. Michael sold the house,

a very pretty little house in the old town, and also on the local postcards, and bought a boat. He went off and sailed into Saint Tropez, a long time before anyone had ever heard of Saint Tropez and lived there for a time. He fell in love with a French girl and they got together and decided to open a restaurant. This coincided with a young Bardot arriving in Saint Tropez; John remembers Michael was on the front page of one of the main newspapers in the south of France. The headline said, "guess what, the best food on the Côte d'Azur is cooked by an Englishman". Ironically, John never did eat there, because the venture didn't last that long, sadly, but apparently the food was really delicious. "But you'd arrive at 9 and probably eat about midnight. And that's what my brother was like, the food would have been perfect but you'd have had to wait for it." He set up a business with the French girlfriend, but being a French national she had 51 per cent of it, because that was the law in France. When they fell out of love, she took the thing away from Michael, so he went back on his boat. He was a very good cook. John remembers with his first wife Bettina, "visiting him on his boat in Saint Tropez and he cooked on the funniest little stove, the most amazing lunch". Sadly, things didn't go great after that venture. "Out of business and out of income, he was beginning to run debts up in Saint Tropez and eventually had to do a runner, in the process of which he got shipwrecked and all his possessions and boat, which was not insured, sank to the bottom off Toulon."

Looking back now, John thinks his mother must have stepped in with funds because suddenly he got a new boat and scuttled down to Port-Vendres on the Mediterranean coast next to Spain, not a streamlined yacht but a kind of fat sensible boat.

In Saint Tropez, Michael met and married another lady who was half Argentinian and they had two sons. That didn't last long and Penny, his wife, settled in Minorca with the younger of the two boys and Michael took to the waterways of Europe with Robert, who had never been to school. He is now a ship's engineer but didn't ever go to school. Michael came back to England with Robert and bought a Scottish trawler, "I remember he was moored in the Thames having a radar fitted to this boat. His new scheme was to go to Sri Lanka and hire himself out to rich tourists and sail them around the Indian Ocean, still with Robert in tow."

However, Michael's scheme nearly came undone when someone, incensed that this poor boy wasn't getting an education, reported him to the education authorities in England. John never found out what the outcome of all that was, but believes that Michael set sail before the radar and everything was working properly and got as far in his trip around the world as Mallorca.

"Now it's all very well beach combing when you are young but he was getting on, and he would have been getting to 70 by then and he hadn't got much money, and in a storm his boat was blown up the beach in Puerto Pollensa. The Spanish navy people would have taken him off, but he hadn't got enough money to pay them, so the boat ended up as part of the scenery on local postcards, this Scottish trawler just sitting there." Eventually, he got afloat, and took it round to the next bay and by this time, John and his sister were funding him. "It was only very small amounts but enough to keep him alive. We felt that from what we had heard, we ought to go out and see him. And there was this boat falling apart at the seams, with a whole lot of cats on board, and the smell was unbelievable, and as far as I know it just settled on the bottom and is still there somewhere."

Showing no signs of slowing down, in his seventies Michael got his 17-year old girlfriend pregnant and decided to get way out of it. There was a boat sailing to the Canaries, so he volunteered as crew and went and settled on the island of Gomera, a small island near Tenerife, very untouristy and lovely. He died sometime afterwards and the local people buried him. John found out when he got a call from the foreign office to inform him of his brother's death. "He had an amazing life, until the end, and that was sad really. The child to the 17-year-old girlfriend, stayed in Spain in Mallorca. God knows what happened to her!" says John.

Meanwhile, Robert has grown up, lives in Minorca, his mum has died since. "He has a really good job there with boats and is charming. He came over for a family wedding the other day. So perhaps you don't need an education. He's really nice."

John's other brother David seemed more straight and uncomplicated when he left the RAF, and was persuaded to go into the Rank family business – flour milling. He went to Deptford mills and humped sacks of flour around. In

John with his family. Left to right: Anne, David, Pussy, John and Michael.
[© 2010 John Coates.]

those days you had to start at the bottom and work your way up – John hated the idea of it. Eventually, David got into an executive position, but considering he was the boss's nephew, John thought it was a pretty miserable life. He also went off with somebody else's wife, called Betty, who was Scottish, but he stayed in the family business.

John's Uncle Jimmy ran the Rank flour business and when he died, he left any of the family working in the mills a quarter of a million pounds. "There were only three or four cousins, nephews to me, in the business. I remember my sister Anne was very upset she didn't get anything. She was already in the movie business, but David got a quarter of a million and quit instantly. He went off with Betty, his quarter of a million, his two sons and bought a house in Scotland, where he became the local squire."

It was very pretty where David settled, West of Stirling, Aberfoyle. He followed his uncle's footsteps in that he went horse racing; he didn't own any horses, but he loved horse racing, did all the northern courses and The Grand National steeplechase.

His other love was alcohol, so he decided he'd get an import license for sherry. He went down to Jerez and met the family who ran a rather unusual and posh sherry called Innocente. He became the exclusive agent in Scotland for the brand and every year was invited down to the vineyards for a holiday.

He then decided he would get into Malt Whisky, which he did. And he became sole agent for Scottish malt whisky sales to Sweden. In those days, probably still the same, liquor was imported through the government in Sweden, but David got to know the boss of the whole thing and was invited every autumn to holiday in Stockholm. So he got his holidays paid for.

Aside from that, if you went and stayed, John recalls they had just the most insanely expensive wines, they had bottles of Chateau Y'Quem, which are a hundred and something pounds nowadays, to have with the strawberries. A kind of bonne viveur, David was into moths and had all the lights and equipment for mothing. There is a David Coates' moth in the museum in Edinburgh – the only one ever caught in the British Isles.

John saw his brother just days before he died. He had come to stay with him in Kent and they had three really good nights, talking and drinking and reminiscing. Sadly, he returned back to his house in Scotland, and he keeled over and died, as suddenly as that, within just a few days of getting back from Kent. He was 58 and died of a brain tumor that no one knew about.

" I had some quite eccentric brothers one way or another. I like to think I am by far the most sensible", John reckons.

29

Retirement! At the Lac de Sainte Croix

John doesn't really do retirement, at least not in the pipe and slippers sense, though he does like to do the odd spot of rose pruning and is a dab hand with a watering can. France, more specifically, his house in Provence, has been an important part of his life since he wound down TVC and in many respects is the fruit of his labours for all the hard work he put in at TVC and before.

The house, a beautiful architecturally designed house just below the village of Aguine, overlooking the Lac de St Croix, is where he is happiest these days. He still loves the area as much today as he did in 1972, when he had first discovered it with Chris all those years ago.

Over time, they had continued to come back, taking a week off here and there and stayed in all sorts of different places around the lake. They got to know the area really well, as they were coming throughout 1972, 1982, 1992 and 2002, and kept talking about buying a house one day, if ever they had the money. In 2003 John had wound down TVC when he suddenly got an offer on the building for a million pounds. John thought, "gosh, I could retire a bit with a million", but felt embarrassed because he would have to tell Ginger (Gibbons of Grand Slamm, who rented part of the building) to get out because "I've been made an offer I can't refuse". John took Ginger out to lunch to explain the situation and sometime later, Ginger said, "I'll match the offer". John accepted and turned down the other offer, though wondering if he was doing the right thing. And bless him, says John, not only was he true to his word and bought the property, but he let John stay on with Norman and Alex (Tham – John's PA at the time) on the top floor.

With this windfall, John's first thought was he could buy a house in France, so he and his youngest daughter went on a trip around the Lac de Sainte Croix to see if they could find a suitable house. During the course of the first trip, they saw the house they eventually bought and fell in love with it. But it was more than John hoped to pay, as he wanted to buy it outright and didn't want a mortgage. He remembers very well that first meeting with the then owners, who brought out a bottle of wine just as they were leaving. John his daughter and the sellers sat on the terrace and had a glass of wine. "We sort of felt they liked us, but I was thinking as we looked at more and more houses it was expensive." Later, they did another scout around. "Like a lot of English, we were looking for a run down farmhouse but never saw one we liked. We saw the one we eventually bought again and short-listed two. One outside Aups and this one." John's elder daughter got to have the final pick: "we showed her the house at Aups and this one. It really is magical and, of course, she chose this house being the more expensive and here we are. I still love the area. The people are charming. My daughters inherited a house in Switzerland, and they remortaged it, and paid for the lovely swimming pool. I think it's just one of those flukey things. Finding this house where Chris and I had dinner all those years ago."

Despite having the house in France, John still keeps busy in media in one capacity or another. "I've sort of pottered around the fringe and done kind of executive producing for people. Quite a bit for Catherine Robbins who's a good friend. I helped her put together the 13 half hour specials of a *Fantastic Flying Journey*, which was a good experience, again working not with Varga but other people in Budapest. They had an Israeli director, who spent part of his time in Israel and part of his time in Budapest. The animation was being done in Korea, and some of it was good, and some of it was pretty uneven."

Though John was pleased overall with the series, there were problems when it aired. "The lady running children's programming at ITV was not getting on very well at that stage, and for reasons that none of us knew, when it was delivered, she ran it out over 13 days instead of 13 weeks in the height of summer in the hottest period of that particular year." The series didn't rate that well, but very little was done to get it an audience. "I think it could have been much more successful, and certainly was miles better than other children's stuff going out that time." After that, Catherine bought the rights to *Pumpkin Moon*, an American book about Halloween. She invited Hilary Ardus who had directed *The Bear* and worked for John for years and years to direct it. The project worked out very well. It was a half hour special that Sky commissioned for Halloween night and it got fantastic reviews and very good ratings when it went out. "The nice people at Sky lunched us soon after and amazingly ordered a follow up, which was a pretty unusual thing to happen, particularly in this day and age when raising money is so difficult."

John also worked as executive producer on a special called *Jack Frost*, produced for the BBC, based on a book of the same name. It was made in 3-D and most of the work was done in India. The production was a good experience for John who grew up in a less technological world and is not well versed in computers – "I didn't even have a mobile phone then. I learnt quite a lot on that production. The film got good reviews and, as far as I know, a good audience, but it should have been a series. Again the BBC, I don't find them very daring, so it was just a one off and that was it."

John doesn't have a studio these days, so asks his friends to do the actual producing and all the hard work. One of these is a script he has had developed for some years called *Whoops*, a story of a blind dog, found wandering the roads of the Dordogne. The dog was kept by Val, one of John's former PAs and a friend. Friends had phoned her up with a horror story about this dog they had found, bedraggled and under nourished and in a fair old state wandering along the roads. On hearing the news, Val had rushed off one afternoon when John was staying with them only to appear some hours later with this little dog. It had been to the vet and been cleaned up and was looking all fluffy and nice. The only thing was when they took it to the vet they discovered it was blind, totally blind. It had no eyes at all. When it arrived at Valerie's house, it couldn't find anything and bumped its way around. John remembers thinking "it was interesting that the resident terrier and two ginger cats didn't really take

John, Nicola and Giulietta enjoy a celebratory glass of champagne, provided by the estate agent, the day they got the key to the house in France. [© 2010 John Coates.]

an awful lot of notice of the dog as he manoeuvred around, bumping into things". By the time they sat down to supper in the little patio they were trying to find a name for him. As they kept going Whoops every time he banged into something, he got called Whoops. Val's husband Barry was a retired agency copywriter, and about a year later, he sent John a script about Whoops saving the day. It was much more suitable for live action than it was for animation so John asked Barry if he could take it over and develop it. Barry agreed and with some input from other quarters, they now have a great script. John raised half the budget some time ago, has a broadcaster lined up, channel 5, but is still missing the other bit of money. "It's a shame because it is really lovely and I think it could be like *The Snowman*, something that kids will want to see again and again. It's based on a true happening but is an invented story but it's fun and quite a number of friends got together." He has the crew already in mind: "Hilary Ardus would direct it, my friend Jerry Hibbert's studio would produce it and everything is sitting there, and nothing". British children's broadcasting is in disarray, and this concerns John, as it does all UK producers. "As of very recently, ITV have stopped producing children's films and the BBC, I have to say, are not very adventurous or amazing, and that's the only place we can now go to raise money. Channel 5, Nick there is marvelous, but their funding is very small. And I have to say I am really

173

disappointed with Channel 4. Camilla Deakin and Ruth Fielding took over for a brief spell, but after that, the commissioning editorship was closed down and C4 hardly do any animation at all now, which is a shame because there are so many marvelous films to be made. There's no imagination, nobody takes risks any longer and I think the poor kids deserve better, not just series of 26 to 52 episodes of mediocrity."

John is not sitting still. Other projects he would like to do include John Burningham's lovely book, *The Magic Bed*, "which I've been developing with my friend Ginger, both as a half hour special and a series of ten minuters". Also, he is helping with another 50 minute special called *Stefan and the Lost Dove* based on a book by Eliane Wilson. "We have done a presentation at the Cartoon Forum in Gerona with splendid illustrations by Pat Gavin who will be directing the film. The story is based on the biblical story of Noah's Ark and the Great Flood. The third dove, the dove of peace, never returned … "Would you believe the money people are of the opinion that peace is not commercial?!"

30

Ethel and Ernest

As the time of writing, John is currently producing his next film, *Ethel and Ernest*, which some say is Raymond's greatest book so far. There is a bit of a convoluted story to how John came to be producing the film. Raymond first gave John the rights, verbally, some years previously in a gentleman's agreement kind of thing. Thrilled, as he loved the book, John hurried off to the BBC to Sophie Turner Lang, then Controller of Programme Acquisitions, who was very enthusiastic about helping him make a film. After talking came the concrete plans and over the course of a year, and many lunches, the BBC agreed to produce with John a television feature, about 90 minutes long.

All was going swimmingly and then bump! Raymond saw a repertory stage production of the book that he had found (a) not very good and (b) had upset him a lot. Seeing his parents characterized on stage was too much for him and he said he'd rather not go ahead with the film – he explained all this to John in a very nice long letter, apologizing for his feelings.

John was obviously disappointed but also quietly determined not to give up. Deep down, he thought people get over these things, so he left it a year or two and asked Raymond again, and Raymond said no … And then, in the summer of 2009, at the Jolly Sportsman, John and Raymond's favourite lunching place, he asked yet again and this time Raymond said, yes, why not.

This time, John got an option agreement from Raymond's agent and already had in mind Roger Mainwood as director; he had directed one of the best Beatrix Potter films amongst other things. Over a very long lunch, John asked Roger if he

Cover of Raymond's book.
[©2010 Jonathan Cape/Random House.]

would like to do it – Roger had animated on almost all of TVC's specials from *The Snowman* on – and Roger went berserk, with delight. "He asked me if I was serious and I said yes, I'm fed up of hanging around", says John. "I'm not able to afford to spend huge sums because I'm using my own money. So he's doing it for a modest rate and then when the money comes he'll get the proper fee."

On the same basis, he's roped in Richard Fawdry, who together with Joan Ashworth did the storyboard on *When the Wind Blows*, based on Jimmy's scribbles from Cannes. The storyboard is now finished and put on to DVD and John

understand why other people wouldn't agree. It seems to me that there can only possibly be one God that's impartial, therefore there can't be a Muslim God, a Jewish God, a Celtic God, and so on and so forth, because it wouldn't make sense and I can't get along with things that don't make sense to me. Talking of sense, what happened to common sense? It seems to me that mankind now relies on computers and has forgotten how to think.

Back to religion: the impartial God doesn't have to be an old man with a beard and however it has been symbolized. It could be something quite different. For instance what's wrong with the Sun? The Sun brings us everything we need and puts us in good humour, grows our food and the vegetation we need to survive. It seems to me as long as the Sun comes up in the morning and goes down in the evening there won't be any major problems on earth. The day it doesn't, is the day I'll worry!

THE END

Index